Suffering In Silence

By Kenneth J. Cody

DEDICATION

This book is dedicated to anyone who has suffered or supports someone affected by a mental disorder. You are not alone. And you no longer have to suffer in silence.

ACKNOWLEDGMENTS

I began writing these poems and journal entries with the idea of one day writing a book, this was the easy part. Actually finishing it, was much more difficult. It took many dark days, reliving many painful memories and reopening old wounds in order to come to this current stage. I have many people I would like to thank, for without them and their support and guidance, this book would not have been made possible.

My close friend, established writer, editor and advisor Kris Lewis.

My daughters Courtney, Mikayla, and Caelyn, for continuing to show me on a daily basis what unconditional love means, without bias, without judgments.

A special thank you to Courtney for her amazing courage and strength and letting me be her daddy forever.

To my son Kenny, for showing me the true meaning of strength through his will to survive.

And lastly, I would like to thank my wife Melissa, because it is with her encouragement and love that I was able to write this book to begin with, realizing that I am who I am and I do not need to feel ashamed.

Table of Contents

Chapter 5: *2000* pg. 105

Chapter 6: *2001* pg. 126

INTRODUCTION

Throughout the course of my life I have had many ups and downs like most of the individuals who walk amongst us. However as the writing in my book depicts, it will appear that I have had more downs then ups. Many with bipolar disorder will seek treatment when they are in a depressive episode and I too can relate to this common phenomenon. This is often the case when it comes to writing macabre poetry.

Poetry to me is a release like no other. It is away for me to be able to dig deep inside the haunted world of my polluted mind and reveal the true skeletons in my closet. There are no rules, no barriers and no judgment. And the best part is in the end there is a sense of cleansing when the piece you are currently working on is finished.

The exception to this rule like with any artist is that your work is never truly finished, especially for an individual who suffers from a mental disorder such as bipolar. I know that though my mood may shift for a few days, weeks or even months, in reality I will be right back where I started and the need to create will continue to be there.

As you read my book you will see that as my moods have shifted, the content and the complexity of my writing have shifted as well. This makes for an interesting time capsule that has been able to capture some of my most intricate feelings and emotions, some at times I did not even remember until I re-read the poem.

I found that I had an infatuation for suicide as well as an underlying self-hatred that encompassed me to use multiple swear words in my early years. The transition of maturity is recognized as you progress through the years that tells me that the creation of this book was successful.

As you read through I only ask that you show a little respect, as these are the most personal thoughts I have ever put down on paper. From my early writing in 1996 to recent times, each and every word is written by me unless noted otherwise.

Chapter 1: 1996

Pain Inside

I can't stand it,
Pain that eats my insides.

Vision of the future,
You as my bride.

All was good,
Now all is bad,

What a rough year,
I have had.

I still feel as you to me,
I am tired of kneeing on my knee.

Why I ask, what shall I do?
It's so hard, hard when I still love you.

THE EVOLUTION OF MY ART*

Over the past 16 years I have been writing and maturing. With every year I have grown and naturally the art I create has grown as well. Looking back I am appalled at the idea of the profanity and word choice I used, however the importance is necessary to the creation of the literary offering. It presents a transition of growth, as my life elevated beyond word and developed from adolescent depression and manifested into the explosion of self -mutilation and the manic rage of bipolar disorder. I mean what exactly is this book about and what am I trying to accomplish here exactly?

I am merely trying to show a pattern of undiagnosed suffering that lead to a major mental breakdown in 2003 that nearly ended my entire existence. This must of manifested from somewhere, and it did. It hid beneath the surface and grew throughout the years. The seeds were placed, as early as 12 years old when the ink first hit the paper, or at least this is the first documented proof. In reality the monster was born earlier when the abuse, silence, anger and sadness started to surface. Unfortunately I kept it hidden and didn't have the courage to write it down.

In the early years of my art I lived inside my head, created false worlds, metaphors and realities. You cannot take them seriously, however they are just as important because most 12 year olds do not normally think this way, however I am one of the few that did. And fortunately I chose to right all my feelings down, in the form of songs and poems.

Godsdecay: a screen name I used between the ages of 13 and 17 years old. It means that we are all gods' children and we are born to die, because as we age we slowly decay.

I am no ashamed to look back and see what kind of darkness I had in my life, or read the words I wrote and feel as though I needed help. My words are beautiful because they are real and pure and full of so much emotion, passion and intensity. Sure I wish I could have opened up more to the people around me, however at the time I didn't, and this book is the final product. I will never stop writing because it is who I am, as a painter who continues to paint.

Untitled

Voices, I hear,
It's all over now,

How did it happen I don't know how?

My legs are limp, my head is light,
All because of our fucked up fight,

I'm sorry, I yell,
But you do not care,
You hiss at me with a confused stare,

I'm sorry,
Please calm down,
You squint eyes and give a frown,

You throw your fist and knee me in the balls,
All in now dead in the dark red halls,

I'm sorry, all is gone.

Fantasy

Some like to be tied up,
That's not that fun,

Others get spanked,
Mr.'s fat gun.

But no,
You have it all wrong.

This isn't a movie,
This isn't a love song.

Love,
A big part,

Sex not just from a dick,
But from a heart.

Give a meaning,
Make sparks,
Don't eat to fast like sharks.

Sex is not all fantasy love...

Sarcastic Hangover

I do not know what happened last night,

I woke up this morning with a wife,

I don't why,

I don't know how come,

She's even pregnant with my son...

ALCOHOL*

My alcohol addiction is something that I am not ashamed of and when asked about will talk openly about. You will find when conducting research that many people suffering from bipolar disorder as well as other mental illnesses, also suffer from addiction issues. My addiction is alcohol.

I started drinking alcohol as a young teenager when I was shy and the need for a quick fix to ease my mind of the social anxieties I encountered were great, alcohol would erase that burden. I enjoyed the taste and would instantly relax becoming a funny man and the life of the party.

I often drank socially for these reasons and when I joined the Army at 17 years old it seemed like alcohol became an all you could eat buffet. The choices were unlimited and with the added stress, the need for the drink grew. At this point it seemed as if I was beginning to feed off the buzz, and as my buzz would begin to disappear I would constantly chase the buzz and started terming myself a buzz chaser.

In 2003 when I had my manic break at the National training center in California while on active duty, my alcohol addiction grew out of control. I found myself drinking nonstop. Alcohol became my best friend. It soothed the pain I felt on a daily basis from the constant torment my military superiors were putting me through. I drank to wake up and I drank to fall asleep.

Bipolar had surfaced and I didn't understand. There were times I would drink and become erratic and extremely manic, and then time where I would drink and grow extremely depressed and suicidal. However the addiction had me and I was losing control. I no longer cared. Alcohol allowed me to be anyone but me; anything became possible while under the influence. In the end I was left with severe alcohol dependency where anytime a stressful situation occurs, anxiety, and even a social event takes place the urge for alcohol is always present.

There are many other substances that have been present in my life that I have used to numb the pain, as I am sure most of us can say the same, alcohol has just been my number on adversary. I have come to the conclusion that this is a battle I will continue to fight until the day I die.

Untitled

Why did you do this to me?
You broke the last limb off me tree,

There's nothing left I hate to say,
A bottle of conditioner and I'm on my way,

No to talk to and nothing for fun,
Except me and my rusty old gun.

You fucked me over and played with my mind,
After all of those times spanking to your behind.

I can't believe this day has come,
You broke my heart,
I love you forever until death due us part.

Her

I look at her when that funny feeling comes,

I can't control it,

I bite my thumbs,

She presses against me,

Our tongues meets,

I don't want it to stop,

She taste so sweet.

All of a sudden thoughts come into my head,

About me her cuddling in bed,

All this all so much for Her

Kurt Cobain

Even though I was young,
When you passed away,
I still remember you,
Along with your unforgettable name

An idol your are to me,
A person in concert I was never be fortunate to see,
You are my hero.

Even though you rest in peace,
From beyond you are,
I pray you will be released.

When I am asked what left-handed guitarist,
I love the most,
Ask for this name and

It will always remain the same.

Kurt Cobain.

CHAPTER 2: 1997

THE MONSTER OF BIPOLAR*

Would you like to know how disgusting this disorder is? If you would then continue to read, and if not please skip ahead to one of the many poems that follow in throughout the body of this book. In June of 2012 I went to the White River Junction Veteran Hospital. I went to the mental health walk in clinic due to being off my medication and suffering from severe manic symptoms. My exact words to the doctor on duty were "I cannot get my brain to slow down".

The next 3 months became a living hell for me as the medication I was prescribed was weaker than the previous bids I has been on. However I had lost a lot of weight and the potential for gaining weight due to stronger medications was great and this was the main factor in the bid choice at the time. Hospitalization was recommended and I declined, as I didn't want to be away from my family.

I was sent in to a tailspin of a severe 3-month mixed episode. During this 3 month mixed episode I had periods of extreme irritability where the monster that I try so hard to hide unfortunately showed himself in his scariest form. When this happens I have multiple out of body experiences. I grow angry and fierce and bite the head off of those closest to me, and sadly Melissa is the one who feels it the most.

She stands her ground and separates the children from these episodes, as I sit in the corner and watch the monster from outside my body move through the house on his tyrant of terror. Lucky for those around him, the monster is not violent he is just verbally abusive. I hate watching him, and I scream at him to stop. However he is too powerful for me and seldom listens to me.

When the monster does finally listen I transition into another emotion, which is usually accompanied by sobbing profusely and multiple cigarette smoking sessions. At this point it is when the craving for alcohol is at its up most intensity however smoking more muffles its strength. Also the monster has now disappeared by now although he is now inside me trying to get out, I hold him in, I feel his anger accompanied by sadness and the feeling is an unbearable struggle.

Am I sad or am I mad and do I live or do I die. This is an example of Dysphoric mania (mixed episode). I would not allow myself to be hospitalized and the kicker is this. I know that there are times that this illness makes me want to completely end my existence. I know it's not me speaking but the disorder or the chemical imbalance in my brain that has taking over. I also know that the love for my wife and kids is so strong that I will fight to stay alive and beat that feeling for as long as it takes.

During the 3 month mixed episode I became extremely suicidal and again hospitalization was recommended. Now this is where the disorder steps out and shakes you hand with it nasty dirty paws. I found that after reading my transcripts from my medical records that I told the doctors that I did not want to be locked up because I would not kill myself due to my wife and children, and if I was separated from my wife and children due to hospitalization I would find a way to kill myself. I had no recollection of saying that, but under Vermont law I was not considered a danger to myself as long as I was not separated from my wife and children, go figure.

Put It To Bed

I cannot help but feel,

The hate bottled up inside.

I can't even seem to blink an eye,

And remove myself from this fate,

I try to hide.

These words they feel so pure,

And no there is no cure,

So kiss me one last time,

Before I say goodbye.

There's a bottle over there,

Drink away the fear,

Touch you sacred touch,

Leave it all alone.

I cannot go one, now that you're gone.

And slit the final wrist, can't get over that kiss...

Reborn and so real,

Buts it's not the way I wanted it to be,

And life is too hard to deal.

The Ultimate High

Today is black,
There is no shadow to hide behind,

Destroy my heart,
How can you be so kind?

Mental fuck feels so good,
Now I run like you know I should.

Put a gun up to my head,
Going to fuck this pain away,

Blow off my motherfucking head
I'm going away today...

I see and image so bare,
A face destroyed without a care,

And feel this anger inside is deep.
Time to die I no longer have to hide.

I see this blood all over your hands,
As if you pulled the trigger yourself,

I cannot realize this pain inside
My tears can no longer cry.

Why do you choose to be like this?

I cannot seem to feel the truth,
I fuck away and erase today.

My soul erases and I die,

Feelings held inside,
Kill myself to say goodbye,
My new lover is suicide.

So say goodbye my fate has erected,
My pain is gone and I'm resurrected,

And bleed no more I'm empty inside,
Can't erase these images inside.

So take my hand in another world,

Sit beside me,

Love me,

You're making a mistake,
And now it's to late,

To close my eyes has become the ultimate high.

I'm calling you Her

I understand that I mean nothing to you,

And I understand that you don't feel for me the
way I feel for you,

I always tell just how much you
mean to me,

But it doesn't seem to matter,

Wish I could make a difference...

And I'm calling,

I'm calling you Her,

And I'm calling; I'm calling you

Her...

So answer me.

I never do anything right.

And I never get things the way you think they
should be,

So come on and help me out,

Constantly locked away,

Stuck in the dark spot of the earth.

With nowhere to go.

Your not right for me and I'm not right for you so,

BANG! SUICIDE!

In these dark times I am stuck,
I must die,
Leave; fly away cause that's what you must want

MARILYN MANSON*

There are very few people in my world that understand the relationship that I have with Marilyn Manson's music. I can comfortably say that for one my wife Melissa, my sister and my mother and father understand, however no one else truly gets its.

As you read through my book and gain knowledge for the sadness and pain I grew up feeling, it is important to know that the one constant in my life was the music of Marilyn Manson. It seemed that for every scenario in my life Marilyn Manson presented me with a song that would help me escape.

I knew I was different, I didn't respond like other kids. Even as a teen I would react differently, I was more emotional. I was more passionate, more intense. I couldn't convey these feelings to my parents, especially my father and it felt like Marilyn Manson was always there for me in some kind of sick and twisted way. His words spoke to me, comforted me, and tucked me in at night.

To this day there has never be a band that has made me feel this way, even though the I do love other music it's not the same. Recently when my wife was in the hospital on strict bed rest due to a complication with the pregnancy for our son, Marilyn Manson's latest album "Born Villain" soothed the pain I felt. There were songs I listened to when I was scared about losing my wife and my son; it is as if the album was written in response to my current situation. I was in severe mania and this album brought me down and I was able to keep it together for my other three children.

As I tackle my life and what it has dealt me in terms of bipolar, mental illness and everyday normalcies, his music plays an intricate part of my existence and adds to the long list of why I am who I am today. I had the opportunity to meet Marilyn Manson and needless to say it was everything I had hopped it would have been. I was able to tell him that I suffered from bipolar disorder and that through the ups and downs of the disorder his music had helped to save my life.

With this disorder I have been through the depths of hell and his music had helped solidify my place in the world. We talked for ten minutes as I let him in and mentions that in my depressive phase his song "The minute of Decay" would help soothe the pain, and while manic "The Reflecting God" would ease my mind. As a whole his song "The long hard road out of hell" summed up my life. Marilyn Manson said that I had rage inside me and that was not necessarily a bad thing because in his opinion its better to be "mad then sad".

I understood exactly what he meant and for a second I felt like we had a connection where we understood one another. The experience was worth a thousand words and a crucial point in my healing. It made me feel like the 16 plus years of being a dedicated fan had been worth it. Mr. Manson then finished the meeting by inscribing his name and the same phrase he spoke to me "Its better to be mad then sad" when signing my Marilyn Manson action figure, it was the perfect climax to an awesome meet and greet. Thank you Melissa for making it happen.

Left to right: (Twiggy, Me and Marilyn Manson 2012).

Age 13: Part. 1

I still wipe the tears away,
I sleep the nights cold and shallow,
The gun directs me where to go...

The veins,
Are blue and cold.
And I cannot stand you.

Need love and a soul,
Need you with me.
I love you more and more,
As far as the eye can see.

I still remember you,
I masturbate your memories.
The gun directs me where to go,

And I cannot stand you...

Age 13: Part. 2

The mascara blinds me,

My eyes not see,

Your words torture me,

Feeling of no longer we,

I'm such a disease.

I feel your presence,

Touching thy breath.

And soft lips of red silhouette.

In a dream where walls disappear,

Looking for you,

Death anger and fear...

Capture thy thought, world of a tear.

Untitled

When you feel that your world was
bright for today,

The woman 's on the corner looking your way,

A passion to relation,

A price you have to pay,

Realizing your life was nothing but fake.

Look at you, remold...

I love you, I'm told...

But their mad you fail.

Sometimes you try to hard,

A life of multiple relations is a little too hard,

You left and caught me off guard.

You left and all too deep scar.

The stars.
Look at those stars,
Look at my scars,

Feast upon my eyes, In 2 years everyone dies.

Untitled

Got me a person,
That I seem to adore,

Still fucked over by this bitch,
My ex-whore.

The light twitches,
Confused and deprived of life,

So sick by the thought upon the thought upon
bodies that lie.

Empty without you,
So stupid what to do.

So numb can't feel my chest,
My fingers on the trigger better
clean up the mess.

Without her I'm through,
Can't make sense to no longer be with you.

Wept Tears

Here I am,
Locked in the closet,

Pain replacing my heart,
A shallow face,
Love for you,
And an empty place where you once were.

You mean so much,
But feel so little,
For I wipe the tears I wept for you.

I feel as if I have died,
Maybe I should have,
Depressed in the corner,

I love you so strong,
But showing so weak,
What do you want me to do?

Life without you makes me feel so sad,
Only if us two could become one,
I would be together again.

Forever when I die I want you with me,
For I will not rest if not so.

Selling Your Soul For Happiness

This world clouded shit,
Upon the world I live.

This evil lurks behind you,
Punishment he has to give.

When all goes to well,
Found yourself in hell,
Sell your soul for as little as possible.

Love seems to lesson,
Hate takes control,
Immature pussies ruining my life,
To pay for their toll.

I just don't seem to understand,
One second were holding hand in hand in hand,
Just don't seem to understand.

At this point in my room alone,
Showing the devil what he wants to be shown.

Pressing his hands to mine,
Sending a chill from my head to my spine.

Showing me a life different from mine,
A life so beautiful won't cost me a dime.

To live with my love all by my side,
All I have to do is commit suicide.

Unwanted Suicide

Look into my eyes,
Tell me what you see,

An unsaved man,
With a helpless plea,

The fear of death and suicide,
A road to hell he soon would ride,

The sky turned black,
Cause death was there,

He looked at the man with a suicide stare,
The man cried and begged for his life,

As death slit the mans throat with his own knife.

No One

There he sits alone,
There he sits by himself,
No one likes him,
No one dares,
Ass kicked everyday,
But no one cares.

Pick pocketed punching bag,
Fucking dip face,
Fucking fag,
Because no one likes him.

One day he will come back,
Whoop your face and kick your ass.

Told that he's different,
Kicked to the curb,
Told he weird,
So he turns to the herb,
Becomes his best friend,
Stay true doper,
Not a care left in the world.

Why do people have to judge him?
All because he's different.

"inspired by a bullied kid at school"

Untitled

My pain evolves from you,
So sick knowing not what to do,
Feel the hate enrage in me,
Cannot wait to see my wrist bleed.

I've seen the pain,
It wears a mask of your face,
Try to say goodbye,
5 more minutes until I die.

I cannot get,
Cannot give in,
Doesn't work,
Then do it again,

And though its all gone I am now gone.

STD's Infected America

Throughout my life I have yet to see what love really is,
A kiss,
A touch,
Even a fuck.

Its seems to not matter,
Society crawls with disease.

Hormones are eating away at my flesh,
My vines grow in two different directions,
Individuality being the root.

For love is nothing but a fuck to me,
Seems true love has not yet found me.

I am lost in STD's,
And I feel my first fuck will be suicide.

Bang! Suicide

What can I say?
I love today,
I don't want to play,
Not in that way!

Surround me,
Pounding me,
Around my finger on the gun holding the trigger.

She saving my life,
pull out the splinters remove the knife letting go.

Finger on the trigger,
My head is getting bigger what do you love yourself?

Burning a hole in my soul,
Bang,
I shot myself.

I love you what can I do trying all so hard,
To late, I pulled the trigger,
My brains are all over the yard.

Burnt a hole in my soul,
Devil are you sure you want it?
Make me your slave ,
Fuck me,
Don't let me ever quit.

Yeah…
I am the devil right hand man,
No time for you now,
Do you understand?

I mean what I say,
I'm going to die today!
Tell her I love you,
Tell her what I'm about to do.   Bang! Suicide…

CHAPTER 3: 1998

WEARING BLACK *

Being depressed is the scariest feeling in the entire world. We do not want to die, at least not all of us. We simply just no longer want to go on feeling the way we currently feel. Especially when we know that the flowers are near, and that true, there is a light at the end of the tunnel. I wear black because it resembles death, something I am scared of. I embrace my fear by identifying with it.

It's not about scaring people; perhaps it's about scaring myself or preventing myself from being scared. I always walked around with a cloud distorting my face, covering my being and distorting my aura.

Therefore, I identify with the absence of light. I did not wake up one day and choose to obsess over horror movies, dark music and wear black clothing. This is my life, a life style that found me and I embraced it. It is my fate, and it is but a coincidence that I suffer from bipolar disorder, a mere coincidence, that is all.

Empty

If only we couldn't feel,
These emotions we call life.
And taste the sour lips,
I no longer taste.
I wish upon my soul,
Repay me for my sins.
Why must I feel so ashamed?
For the person I am and becoming?

I can no longer look at what makes me happy,
Wanting it and never getting it,
Just takes the last piece ofmy heart away.

I have no heart,
I have no soul,
I am empty.

The Center of my Sore

To open up my heart once more,
The truth behind my failure,
The center of my sore.

A place at once broken,
From lies and sour kiss,
To no longer feel emotion,
Is the wish in which I wish.

Threw this pain of us fuck,
Love thought to be made.
To feel no meaning for our love,
To have nothing left to say...

We must never be together,
I will be broken from today until forever,

Remember I love you.

Blue Skies

I cam at a time when there were blue skies,

I remember the time,

To leave they say goodbye.

That's when life was so fine,

I was never alone most of the time,

Until…

One Day

There is this series of pain filled aggression,
Trying to win this battle against depression,

Series of souls leaves and exit threw sinful doorways.

And I just wish for one day I could be him,
And I could see how it is to feel good from within.

My wrists at times are weak,
Vanishing with every cut,
So sickened and I'm scared to speak,
Now I'm lost in a rut.

And I just wish for one day I could be him,
And I could see how it is to feel good from within.

Shedding Skin

These sleepless nights I lay alone,
How can it be on my own?
These days we look past,
My emotions unreal it's too hard to grasp.

My skin is gone; I'm melting past these days,
    My skin is now gone, please somebody show me the
ways.

    We grew up in a world I was never accepted,
    You were there unexpected,
    But what I am and have become,
    You helped create,
    The perfect sun,

    My skin is now gone, only black remains,
    Trying to wash away all of those stains,
    I am left here with no remains.

Tears for you

Oh how I lay in my bed,
With the tears for you running down my cheeks,
For you gave me strength,
And I may take down the revolver I pressed against my
forehead.

I think of how great it's going to be with us two as one,
Oh how I kiss you and taste the blood that runs through your
veins,

I once was dead but now I'm alive,
Your love has awoken me from hell,
And I may regain my journey I once started.
This dark world has brought us together and the sun will rise
again.

The first three days

There's something cold in this place where I lie,
Its so cold it sends a shiver down my spine,

I can only feel the tingle of my own touch,
And my soul is now lonely.

If I were to call out no one would hear me,
Just left in this world with no one but myself.

When talking to a person is like talking to a wall,
I am introduced to the wall but nothing or no one else.

My music soothes me most of the time,
But I can't erase the memories I left behind.

A tale of intercourse to the ultimate high,
Finding myself the saying goodbye.

The room with familiar faces has now disappeared.
Its time to say hello to a new life and a new year.

Hello 1999.

What keeps me alive?

My pain is the loss of what once was a soul,
To feel the barrel upon my lips,
This feeling I want so much more.
A sudden blow, my life it strips.

Desperate feelings I can't help but feel,
My present is paved with shadow day.
To feel this love is all too real.
To fear a relation when it comes your way.

A time of tears where I thought all end,
You're my heart with open mind,
By the text of your touch my soul had descend.
My eyes were now dry and for once I was fine.

You are the sun that makes me rise,
I pass behind my false goodbyes.

A tattoo to remind you

The eyes that are mine,
Close to the shadow left by the one who I once loved,
My guilt for the lust one directed towards you,
And the flem of my seed infecting your body.

A sad mistake at point where in the mind I was so young and
excited about fornication,

Where really I was just a boy lost in your lost in your insults,
Whipped by your cream that took me away.

You made me feel as if a failure,
Wanting me for nothing but your happiness,
To fulfill the pleasure you felt you deserved,

You were the one I loved.
Shared my secrets with,
But underneath you skin you're just a whore,
Permanently infected with a tattoo of my seed to remind you.

Growing Distant

Hide behind your sorrow,
The face deaf and dark.

Tears hide the eyes of what once was you,
Afraid to see what tomorrow will bring,
Life is at its point a suicide devise,
To love one such as you,
Appears uneasy as it seems.

The tangibility is bad,
Slipping through the tips of my touch.
The microscopic organism crawling into you,
Trying to get close to the sweet skin you posses.

Pushing me away,
Step to another step,
And now I realize the trigger has been squeezed.

Pale Face

The dampness has drowned me,
My eyes at a point where they no longer can see,
The face of answer,
Of which has saved me from this.

My world has turned gray from the black it once was.

I can see the pale faces of those who feel pain,
I have a pale face,
Mostly built from the shame I have suffered from on numerous
occasions.

Opinions all too negative,
Towards the individuality see ked by abnormal characters,
I ask, "What is right? And what is wrong"?

?

this is what you showed me,
false lies hoping to set me free.

Love and lust to fill my open wombs,
Listen to me,
Others are not always what they assume.

Lets slide up to one another,
Know this feeling won't last forever.

PAIN!

Why do you do this,
To me?

False accusations your to blind to see,
What exactly do you me?

Sour Kiss

Dream of first sight,
Reality sum of pain,
Us two in whole and I kiss your sweet lips.

What it closely, I'm floating away…

Feeding breath of air,
Choking on his lung,
Shower of your sins,
Awake because it's all a dream alone.

To be alone

I recall the last thing you said even though it was hard to
understand,
      Why do you doubt the things I do,
      And never really caring why?

And I seem to feel like a mistake was made, not knowing what
went wrong, a pain I can't escape.
      I'm drowned by these tears,
      And decaying by the sand.

      It doesn't get better,
      My days grow dark and I cannot seem to feel.

Going to Hell

I'm dying slowly,
Fading away like a candles wick,
You're across the way looking at me,
The devils grin,
I soon will see.

Why on earth has he come for me.

I have moved away from a place far from here,
A place of hot coals,
Torture and fear,
Goodbye.

Unprotected Disease

So disturbed unsatisfied,
Look all around you,
Before it's your time to die.

The disease seeks you out,
Crawling up filled with doubt,
Protection has once crossed your mind,
Unprotected fantasy full fill being so kind.

Your first time,
Time I guess to remember,
To love your partner,

Never surrender,

Alone in your room,
Sex is the thought,'
To do it unprotected disease you have bought.

Untitled Suicide

The wheels are turning,
As the engines burning
 For death is here.

He knows your name and your life history,
For he is hell,
The fearful ministry,
No, no you cry.

Death is here now its time to die,
Pull out the noose its suicide,
A cry a whisper,
A hallow noise,
Locked in the basement with all your toys.

Standing on the stool and cry aloud,
"Look at me devil, am I doing you proud"?
Shake my hand and take a bow,
Good night, farewell, then my neck snaps now.

Swollen Porno

I play the game but I don't really like it,
Talk is cheap on a flesh eating diet,
Arms of scars I do not show them,
Blood soak stains,
They seep right through it.

I feel the pity of your cries,
I watch the world end eaten by flies.

I play the game,
And I start to like it,
Sick and tired of the commercialism shit.

Pick of the pieces,
And glue them together,
Where ever I walk,
Surrounded by dirty weather.

A dream in Hell

My eyes cast a shadow from the dreams of heaven,
They reflect into a pool of sperm where everyone is infected.

A P marks the spots,
Tattooed on the shoulders of societies beast we call aids,
Orgies occurs frequently,
Where sometimes unwanted by some involving both sexes.

The light is dim,
Revealing blood stained carpets,
Where rodents' known as patients smears their faces in blood,
After cutting themselves.

A room of P marked people having sex,
Inflicting wounds,
Playing self-mutilation card games.

A place where no one gets out alive.

Engraved Erection

When sex turns to lies,
Sour blinded virgins,
We hate cheat shit,
Cut blade kill the surgeons.

God is dead,
No time for a reason,
For me is winter,
The coldest darkest season.

Why is this life going slowly?
We hate and we really try,
When all is over,
Begging slowly,
Your know its your time to die.

When the lies right beside you,
Feeling regret and sorrow,
Kill death in mind,
What a dead sad tomorrow.

We all try a little to hard to poison the demons in your mind.

High off STDs

Your face is like an answer to the problems that lurk our way,
A body to be angry,
To take the pain away.

A slit in your throat,
To brighten up your day,
In your suicide note you have nothing left to say.

This is the way we do it this way,
Tears in your eyes,
Check to see if you're ok,
Death lurks between your legs,
A slut in which they say,
When you die of aids,
You learn it was never ok.

Your cloud ruins the night as the stars brighten up the sky,
Hidden by the scars, trying to keep them out of sight.

Your manhood has evaporated from the disease you have
bought,
Next time listen to the infomercial,
What out before death gets caught.

Random thoughts *

1

My life just slips right before my eyes and I feel dead
And I know you won't remember me,
When I'm thinking knowing you don't care for me.
And even through my eyes they try so hard to see,
My pain,
My fear and anguish,
I keep locked in me,
Can never be spoken.
She wants me,
He hates me,
I try so fucking hard to erase me.

2

How could I love someone who never cared about me?
I couldn't figure out why I miss the ones who hate me.
I spend sleepless nights for the ones I leave,
These bulging eyes it's hard to see.
But I remember the one, who destroyed my insides,
Broke me in two,
Feeling as if I'm forever lost.

3

Are we destined to find someone?
A person to hold,
A person to be comforted by when the sickness has taken control?
I always felt like a disease,
A walking corpse yearning to die,
I know now it's all to possible.

Hello Teenage Suicide

My life seems to go away,
My life just seems to wash away.

My life is tormenting me,
My life has had its last plea.

Controversial corpses spinning a spider web,
To take my life a way.

My life has trouble me,
I am trying so hard,
By myself sobbing.

I once thought in my head,
As I pull the trigger,
To late I am now dead.

Slide Away

Hello there this is more like it,
Beaten and abused,
I can't deny it.

I masturbate your memory but I forget to climax,
My bodies all destroyed in the burning haystacks.

See the drugs that you take,
Trying to help was my biggest mistake,
Now you're gone,
We no longer have each other,
Soon you will see,
You will be dead in the gutter,

Beaten and blue,
Teeth a chatter,
You think it's over,
But you're wrong,
Life is here,
Staying long.

Going Away Far

Please remember me for the person I be,
A lover with no more dignity,
A person who loved something said to be wrong,
A person who always muttered the words to his song.

And its wrong people have to be this way,
And I'm lost,
Stuck in the minute of decay.

And when you cry don't think of me,
And when you want to die,
Remember me,
Because I was there when it counted.

When you love you cannot live,
And when you're sorry,
It's hard to forgive,
And when you're happy cause the time has come,

Turn around because what's done is done.

Something said, but not worth saying

I try not to remember the pain of depression,
I try to forget those eager trips of regression,
I see the stars shine so bright,
They make an indention in my eyes.

But I do not remember the last time you said hello,
Need to love, something you do not know,
But you told me to go away,
Away from you,
Me and everybody,

Something said but not worth saying,
The maggots are on the knees and they've started praying,
Jesus goes away,
And I am loving, loving today.

And I don't remember when you use to care,
I'm left alone where its cold and my skin is bear.
Your cross keeps holding me down,
And the maggots keep causing the sound.

Random thoughts 2*

1

Night breezes air,
Filtering the blackened room,
Peeking through the blinds,
A blue light revealing our silhouette bodies,
Collapsed together.

The night is dead,
Surrounded by unrevealed noise,
I awake for was this a dream,
A first breath,
A feeling of relief and empty once more.

2

The feelings from within,
Pondering the mind of a confused soul,
Realizing all that has failed has left great hold on your heart.

How much more should go on,
To take a little is all too much,
A person to hold,
Screw and emotionally drain,
The remains of me locked away from all to see,
To terrified to reveal my true self.

Tortured by you

I had a dream that filled my head blue,
Undergo some treatment,
If only you knew.

But the gun is weighing me down,
The perfect suicide frown,
Arming up with no reason,
To stop this compulsion from coming down.

There is no way to cut each and every vein,
Before it's too late,
And now there's no pain.
I want to die knowing I cannot be normal.
I want you to witness the end you have caused.

Never Free

I can see, I try to see with eyes that are blind,
I can feel, feel my soul begin to unwind,

Even though the pains on hold,
My soul must have already been sold.

Though the sky is dark from yesterday,
I try to hide,
Oh what a beautiful Sunday,

My systems low,
My urge has been overflown,
By the creatures that we know as demons,
With your cross in hand, I can't begin to stand.
And this is my end.

Contaminated Soil

My heart grows empty,
Thinking to myself,
Feel the horror and pain of suicide inside me.

Moving on to a place where the sun shines,
Maybe they will dry the tears I cry, please go away.

This world has that we live have thrown me away.

Now that I'm empty and see that you don't care,
These weeds that hold me down,
You cannot begin to realize that they are there,
So cut me free.

Man made of stars

I feel as if my body has been lost in this place we call earth,
The stars soothe me,
For I became the star man,
The man from outer space.

And even though I'm wrong I am loving every minute of it,
Loving this new face of pain.

I'm from space,
And in space,
Sometimes I feel this way,
When you tell me I'm wrong.

In space, in space it's draped in a black cloth,
As if I'm dreaming,
Do you know what it's like to feel the pain and know there is
no god?

The undecided

The undecided doesn't understand,
Did you ask the question correctly?
Just take my hand,
And I will guide you through this hell to be,
The world soon will come to an end;
You will see.

From the heavens above who no longer want me,
Don't ever forget who I am,
Because you may be the last person I am able to see.

I hurt feeling this way,
And I'm scarring myself,
The undecided must go,
Leave me on my own.
A love song suicide.

And I cry,
And I decay,
My body begins to die.

Don't know what to do,
I scrape myself away,
Burning my eyes,
Cutting my veins,
Nothing left to feel,
The undecided breaks his deal,
And passes away.

S.U.I.C.I.D.E. (Rap/Rock Song)

Coming from the death,
Shoot yourself I bet
But those niggas on the west
With their fucked up type of dress

Being played like a fool
Gun in your face, back to the old school
Big boy
Breaking all the rules
All feeling good as were high
Trying to live the life that we all should be living by.

This is how it is
So this is how it is
Life is a bitch
We cover up!

You better grab your gat
with that shit that you pack
because they're coming to get you
for a matter of fact
got my girl in this hell where I lie,
from the heat that I feel
trying to find a place to hide.

CHAPTER 4: 1999

FAMILY*

My family is the backbone of my life. They are the reason I made it home from the Army after suffering the manic break where my bipolar disorder decided to show its ugly face. And I would like to thank my mother and father for their unconditional support with bringing me home. They never gave up on me and spent countless hours and resources fighting with the chain of command that damn near killed me out in Ft. Riley Kansas.

In recent times my family has grown and remains the backbone behind my existence, and to them I am grateful. My wife Melissa has loved and supported me from the moment we met, and living with a person who suffers from bipolar disorder is no walk in the park to say the least. She is a pioneer, a wonderful wife and mother to our four beautiful children. The ups and downs to this disorder have not only put a strain on my well being but have also put a strain on Melissa as well. However her strength goes unchallenged, as she has been able to maintain our home through my rapid mood changes. Our children who our too young to comprehend such a complex disorder have no idea of the turmoil their daddy deals with on a daily basis and I have Melissa to thank for this.

I have spent countless days, weeks and months of my life toying with the idea of no longer being a part of it. This unfortunately is part of the downside of going through the lows of bipolar disorder. The one thing that has always made it possible for me to be able to go to sleep and wake up to breath another day is my family. I know that the lows will not last forever, and that I have so much more to offer the world as well as life to share with my children. Melissa and I have a saying and I will take this time to share it.

The saying is "We did not get married and start a family to raise these children alone". We have goals and a future planned and that future involves both of our children and us. In closing I would like to say that I am thankful for my wife Melissa and our four beautiful children Courtney, Mikayla, Caelyn and Kenny for loving me and supplying me with the air that I breathe.

I would like to thank my father Keith Cody and Mother Kelly Cody, sister Erin and brother Eric for their support. I would also like to thank my second set of parents David and Polly Gundry for taking me on as a son and excepting me for me, the whole package. Thank you both.

Bully

Why must I fear you?
This morph of a man,
Who eats dignity to arouse ones self.

He creams at your discomfort,
Portraying him to be the man,
For he sucks your confidence to satisfy his own.

A hypocritical stain,
In which is suppose to go away.

I know nothing of this person,
Except the insults he writes my name on.

He's a true servant to popularity,
Performing oral sex upon its custom,
He has no dignity,
He is no one important,
He is nothing.

I

My feelings are lost,
As if trying to find,
Shattered the pain,
From what I left behind,
It never gets better,
The days begin to grow short,
Locked away lonely,
Feelings of exhort.

What have I done,
To feel a loss,
Please go away,
If it's my life it must cost.

Feed upon me,
And remove this pain,
A feeling of not being wanted,
A toxic little stain.

For I am not
What you believe,
I will grow to be something,
Just wait and see.

Random Thoughts*

1

As I sort of unwind and try to cope with the person I am,
These feelings all caused by the simple loss of my innocence.

How can the being sworn to love and care for my existence
place insanity in the tips of my fingers,

Like a downward spiral,
Slowly taking me down,
As I lay latched to it.

It slowly drags me raping myself confidence and emotions,
How can I be the cause of such vulgar displays?
A walking bomb waiting to explode,
Well they get what they want when I'm gone.

2

Crazy for a day,
Awake in a fog dead to the world,
A pain piercing tiny holes in my stomach,
Causing tears to fill these hollow eyes.

Hidden happiness for the day,
Torment thy peers only to satisfy my twisted want,
To feel shit and step into my shoes.

To see the hurt I cause,
Only wish of death departure and suicidal fantasizes,
To end the hurt and pain I have caused.
Don't cry because of me.

A bunch of mumble

You're right here with me,
My heart is where you lie,
To nurture my heart live,
To help me stay alive.

Never knowing just when I will heal,
I feel I have lost you,
You nearly saved me from absolute hell,
But now you have left,
It is not the first time this has happened,
Though I thought it would have been the last.
Why do I continue to do this to myself,
Put myself through the burden of this,
I will have my answers as soon as I die.

A last goodbye

I see the hurt in your eyes,
I quiver to hear your soft cries,
I cannot help but feel this way,
With nothing left I have gone away.

The sadness has destroyed me,
My tears of rage but you ignore me,
I no longer can take the burden of this pressure,
Lost in the clouded images of the hidden treasure.

POW!

I have seen past you,
Destroy my rebirth and start over,
However they have also destroyed the earth.

Impossible.

I am nothing

I feel as if the everlasting stitch will never cease and desist,
How it haunts me like a lost soul on its way to hell.
Dragged through this life a chain attached to my shaven throat,
Each days like another grasp for air,
But the days grow darker,
And I begin to feel numb.
As if my soul has been sold,
My heart destroyed right before my eyes.
My mentality is certified to fit you,
To totally ponder the day at the bottom of your feet,
To answer your command for a token of being loved,
I am foul, I am nothing.

Suicide Embrace

Night passes by through midnight gloom,
Power of the day through graveyard tomb,

Empty souls yearning for something with no known cause,
Shedding tears of night upon the headstone yards.

Glimpsing up to the sky,
Pondering the many thoughts of why,
Alone wondering in a daze,
As the time graciously passes by.

The tomb is filling with gloom,
Inside the empty souls are yearning for someone,
Goodbye.

The headstones releasing a mist,
The empty souls remove their wrist.
It's time to die.

Mumbles*

-This day flies right through my veins,
Turning in my sheets covering up the stains.

-The end of the road is painted with pretty faces,
To heal up all your fears,
Everything your mind disgraces,
To slit the veins in every wrist,
To lust over temptation,
Sex in which you can't resist.

-Do you feel this pain,
Feel this fate crawl through your fingers,
Your heart pound,
And your eyes swell?
In a state where nothing else matters except death.
Nothing but padded walls surrounding you.
For the hair you have becomes the hair of the beast.
For he is taking over you,
And you must run.
From the beast,
And run from the fate he brings with him.

-Envy

I glimpse upon the light,
These tears mold my eyes,
Struggle to cope the balance,
To end the fray of fright.

This pain how it sticks with me.

-why must I cope this way,
My wombs fail to heal today,
And even though I try,
I am never going to be the right way,

I feel there's no release,
To say goodbye, And pull the last string.

> -*Rozz Williams*: I wait to hear what next you will say,
> Anticipate your worlds, I say them everyday, tears fill
> my eyes as I read about your life, ask the question why,
> did you have to take your life? I push the play to hear
> your voice, I dim the lights in memory of you.

End of the world

You see the world an image in mind,
A bundle of flames at the end of time,
Voices and screams ponder the air,
Vow, distinct and toxic despair.

Corpses, debris paves your walkway,
Shedding tears as if this were your last day.

Reach out for the one you love,
Collapsing to see a puddle,
Huddled around by one bloodstained dove.

There's nothing to do except die at your time,
Radiation heartbeat feeling divine,
Some will die first and some will die last,
The year 2000 has just now past.

Shattered Pain

Shattered pain I can't help but feel,
A vision a vision in eyes if only to heal.

I am nothing that matters in life,
If time to die they would offer a knife.
Tie the noose and load the gun.
Ask me to try it as if suicide were fun.

An empty surrounding my body would lie,
Alone and shivered amongst the decay,
Gone and the reflection is bare,
When ending my life you didn't care.

Vision of the dead

Vision of the dead upon these eyes,
Sitting in the back enduring your lies,
Visions of the future as time goes by,
Leave so fast and don't know why.

I never meant much just a stain,
Barely alive feeling your pain.
Barely equipped what's left to gain,
Nothing but lies and your pain.

No longer exist

Sometimes I fade away,
From the ignorant fools that bleed my day,
I focus in as I am right and those who are wrong,
Though no longer in sight,
My wrist have bled,
No more can bleed,
As if ending my life,
We're doing a deed,
The night has become pure as oneself,
I'm left cold,
Though I have now changed,
But my image must remold.

CHAPTER 5: 2000

Fuck Everything

I have no soul,
I have no sin,
Fuck this world we are living in.

Fuck those bastards,
Who don't give a fuck,
And fuck stress directed upon us.

Fuck this sacrifice we call our savior,
And fuck those hypocrites that say Fuck!

Change of heart

I fumble through those pages the form the shape of a heart,
And my veins pump blood,
Though I know I shouldn't cut,
The pages are black as if burnt over a long period of time.

To which person shall it be, who, or me
For these eyes are swollen and can no longer see,

My only feeling is love I sure know,
Who puts the S in suicide?
And whose fault must it be if it is I?

Restrained

Try to compromise can't seem to realize,
What I was and become,
I can't control it; I can't seem to let go of the gun.

It's been here so long this feeling like this,
The fire in my heart that I can't seem to put out.

This is not enough,
This world will destroy you,
It's they, who no longer allow you to feel,
So I have no choice,
I have to kill it all away.

Because I've been broken since day one,
And there's nowhere else to go.

My Bloody Valentine

Time has past,

This is the last,

Time was spent,

And now it's gone,

So sick of the rut,

A hallmark holiday,

To say goodbye,

Because alone again it is for me,

Bleeding and a wonderful day to die.

Thoughts*

-And I'm sad,
This feeling is me,
I can't believe it's close to the end,
Not knowing what I will do, or where I will go.

I can't erase the feelings that consume me,
I can't erase what I already left behind.

I sit and begin to think what it will be like as I die.

I cannot begin to understand.

-You feel as if the path has gone away for the day,
to decide which way to decide which way to live,
what an impression you seem to give,

so I miss you departed satanic ways,
I'll never see you for the remainder of my days,

Ending in divine.

Make him go away

Siting in my space,
Thumbing through the papers of my life,
Rekindling the thoughts I wrote,
And I'm scared to see if wrote he said is true.
And I'm scared to be alone.

I look past his remarks,
A petty fucking fuck,
I don't know what to do,
But god I want to kill him.

I want my life back,
My self-confidence,
I want to erase the burden of this,

Maybe it will all go away.

For you, but why

It's almost two, I cannot see,
There's a picture of you and it's fading away,
\Why do these feelings come at the wrong time,
I ask why do they come?

Why did I try to make you happy?
Cutting each and every vein to make you smile,
Why did I die to make you happy?
Nothing left to cut now where's your smile.

I can't believe that I contemplated this,
Taking away my life for you,
And I just can't see,
And I'm get weak,
Why?

Watch the tears fall

Look up to the sky,
Feel the bugs fucking pain,
Warm shadow fashion show,
The hate blows away.

Feel a burden as if something,
Bothering you bored out of your mind,
As you watch the tears fall.

No one to relate to

I have been lost since the very first day,
The moment I walked amongst the decay,
Loosing a friend for no good reason,
As if I grew cold a dark new season.

My body had sunk into depression,
Gripping my wrist holding back aggression,
I miss the times at cemetery walls,
Posing in dresses in our friends halls,

Powdering our noses for Manson's show,
Meant so much to me you will never know,
Keeping me balanced from suicide dreams,
Knowing true evil is not what it seems.

Respecting me and the image I hold,
A friend is forever I once was told,
My suicide dreams have not all been past,
My first and only best friend now my last.

Urine Sample

There you are pleasing the man,
Slut you are,
Whore to this land.

A disease ridden scum,
Polluting the air,
Passing your trash with you toxic smell,

Golden bitch,
Get a life.

Stalker

The torment that I'm suffering,
Envision of you departed from all else,
But the persons in which I adore.
How you lay this grief upon my shoulders.

Not even befriending you or ever graced your presence.
At a time where the sun had shined.

To them you are nothing,
But an ignorant ignorance,
They hope to get rid of.

But if all filled with dislike for you,
I must dream for what that must feel.
For I am in debt with sorrow,
But these feelings are still that of hatred
in hope for you to depart their circle.

Coping with you

Close my eyes to what's not real,
Drain my sores never seem to heal,
Forgive me time has ticked away,
To afraid to stay.

I've been here before,
For you I must adore,
And never awake its more then I can take,
I feel the blade upon my wrist,
An urge so hard to resist,
A knot so tight upon the rope,
Struggling trying to cope,
With this.

Emotionless

The thing in fear is fear itself,
My knuckles bled for another day,
These bloody tears will not go away,
And there's no more anyone can say.

I'm afraid of what's in my head,
Tiny visions of the dead,
And the noise keeps killing me,
Bleeding eyes.

My emotions weak just another day,
My heart now melts slowly into decay.

Pro-Death

Try so hard to be free,
Until my death of no longer me,
Cannot control the burden of he,
Feeling around blinded by see,
Searching for a soul of wanting to be,
And beg to stop as if in plea,
A rotting fetus that cannot be me,
Though a choice hard to believe.

This is life why pass it by,
Read your holy book,
And choose the lie,
Freedom is choice so let it ring,
First pro-life then see what you bring.

Kenneth J. Cody

Left Alone

I have broken away from what I felt attached to,
So empty and I am cold,
Oh I remember you digging in me,
And I fall away.

You kept telling me I was special,
And you walked away.

Untitled

I recall the last thing that you said,
Even though it was hard to understand,

Why do you doubt the things I do,
And never really caring why,
And I seem to feel like a mistake was made,
Not knowing what went wrong,
A pain I can't escape,

I've drowned by these tears and rotting by the beach,
Slowly dying.

Afraid of today

I chose to live this way,
Rewriting everyday,
Afraid don't know what to say,
What if this doesn't go away?

I'm not saying I want to die,
Why do I stress to know why,
Feel I'll never be as fly,
To afraid to say goodbye.

I want to live but not this way,
I feel the pain make it go away,
Why do I do this to myself?

I always plan my day,
Always the same exact way,

One bullet to clear today,
To take the pain far away,
To relieve this feeling from insane,
To relieve the pressure by exploding my brain.

A change in the sky

I try to look past these days,
Try to be amazed,
Try to see,
That you are too good to be true,
Try to grasp the thought of being happy.

Is the sky changing,
Is the guilt diminishing,
Or is this reality playing games?

Has the sky opened up,
Am I feeling real or another game,
Is the torment being erased and changing for the better,
Or am I living my nightmare all over again.

6000 miles from heaven

Talking to myself and I felt lonely,
Because I seemed to be in hell,
Heaven so far…
The crosses have weighed me down,
Jesus has forgotten about me,
The lies that you told me,
And the truth has set me free.

All so far…

On my way down to hell.

Anti- Social

I feel as if I can no longer say goodbye,
Please pleasure me on my way down to die,
     I never wanted this you have become the center of my
hate,
     Time to step up and shake hands with your fate.

Look what you have made of me,
I am what you have grown to despise,
Should have taken my kind gesture,
You could stand the pressure.
Mute.

CHAPTER 6: 2001

Hollow

My soul lays sold,
And my heart lays broken,
As if a hammer has destroyed my insides.

I don't understand life,
A game with no directions.

The hands I have,
Had never been touched.

Love such an outspoken thing,
So in spoken I have yet experienced,
I must get use to it.

Feeling Numb

We walk around our heads lost in the clouds of unrealistic
visions,
A picture of life so perfect, so beautiful, so right.

We fool ourselves each and everyday when the truth is
revealed and its power so strong you cannot begin to grasp it.

You fade away loosing emotion,
Reality on life and yourself,
Each days a struggle pleading with yourself to stay alive,

To keep yourself pure,
And hold back thoughts that fuel you for suicide.

You might get use to the feeling of pain,
So much pain,
That death is now beautiful.

Book of lies

To busy to heal from this experience,
Try to be perfect destroyed my innocence,

Now that it's almost time to say goodbye,
I want to tell you I know that you lied.

I read your book and it was a book of lies,
When you laugh it becomes no surprise,
It rips the skins from my bones,
And buries me beneath the throne of each page.

Scared by the night

The night was light shadows,
A million figures wrapped all in one,
Awaken by the remembrance of you,
A heart pounding as if a fist thumping my chest.

I no longer can take being alone,
Frightened by the images in my head,
Scaring me and the sweat rolls off my forehead.

Another nightmare,
No one to call out to,
Like a little kid however now a man,
I must fight this fear on my own.

CHAPTER 7: 2002

NATONTIONAL TRAINING CENTER*

Bipolar disorder surfaced in February 2003 while I was with my battalion in California at the National training Center at Fort Irwin California. We had been under heavy stress preparing for "war games" to take place in the 100 plus degree desert temperature. I knew my job and I knew it well and with this kind of knowledge came great responsibility. I had been up for over 20 hours and the sleep deprivation had been getting to me, not to mention for the past few weeks I had be secretly suffering with what later was determined to be my first real depressive low.

As the stress grew so did the racing thoughts I had been having, which were flying through my head at what felt like a thousand miles an hour until one fateful night when everything blew up. I completely snapped and erupted into a monster. I started talking extremely fast, faster then usual. I couldn't sleep and I was snapping at everyone. I spent the entire night listening to music and smoking cigarettes, putting them out on my arms in the process.

The next day was worse and I awoke and fulfilled my daily soldier duties but the pressure grew until I truly reached my breaking point and all hell broke loose. I began to shout, holler and sob. I made an emergency phone call to my parents where it seemed like every racing thought I was having came to a head. I brought out everything I was currently dealing with and even things that I had held in for year's prior, I could not get the thoughts to stop pouring out. The feeling was absolutely horrible and I did not know what to do so I was referred to Fort Irwin's mental health facility.

In true US Army fashion, it was passed off as a young soldier being away from home and not wanting to go out into the desert, obviously this was not the case. It was suggested to me that upon my arrival back to Fort Riley that I immediately be take to the mental health clinic there for follow up treatment. I then went to the field with my unit. When in the field with my unit I was a complete mess and in a state of mania which at the time I was not aware.

I was irritable, and extremely agitated. One night I told my Lieutenant that I was going to beat the living shit out of him for looking at me wrong. In a heat of rage I drove off with the track vehicle loosing half of the gear in the trailer that was attached, this went unreported because my chief was not in the vehicle and he didn't want to get reprimanded for allowing me to operate without him. I also told another officer he was a piece of shit. The list goes on about the out of character actions I performed while suffering my manic break, however no one seemed to help me but instead threatened me with punishment.

When my battalion did finally return home from the National training center I was forgotten about. I had to walk myself to mental health. My original diagnosis was in fact Bipolar NOS and was told that I needed help outside of the Army. This started the end of my Army life and began the worst day of my life. My chain of command turned their back on me and made me out to be a liar, a psycho and a joke.

I became the subject of numerous taunts and threats and ridicule. One night when I couldn't sleep due to the mania I tried to knock myself out by ramming my head into a wall locker, I was crazy they said instead of getting me help. They threatened my life and said I was faking it, and said that because I no longer wanted to live I would mind going to Iraq and stepping in front of a few bullets for them to save some lives. Needless to say I was soon after discharged from the US Army. However upon my Honorable discharge from the US Army, my medical record had been misplaced and my diagnoses had been changed to Borderline Personality Disorder and Adjustment Disorder.

As soon as I was released from the Army I immediately went to the VA hospital and had my diagnoses properly reestablish to its proper status. I have since learned that the Department of Defense has been under investigation for falsifying diagnoses in order to get out of potentially paying soldiers pensions. What happened to me has also happened to over 31000 other military personnel. As of the publishing of this book my discharge is being investigated by my Senators and Congressman.

A wall of sadness: (Painted By Fear).

I sifted through the ashes of my life,
I pondered this world I tried so hard to erase,
I've felt the fear, the pain of you,
And I have conquered your surrogate mother.

So erase me from this scene,
Crippled in black; decaying from within.
So save me from myself, a tiny little pill to cage the burden of
he.

I can't seem to calm these bulging veins,
I seem to be a little infected,
I've taken the pill in hopes of a new life,
And I am mutilated all over again.

Why, I ask?

Was I born to live in agony?
Tortured from inside as I squirm throughout the outside.
A tension building,
Manufacturing a twitch.

Someone save me! For I cannot save myself...

So hear me when I call out, trying so hard to scale this wall.
So listen to me when I need you,
Cause feeling alone is causing this fear.

Heading Down

Has my life come to an end,
Have I come to the light with an arrow pointing down?

Did you enjoy making me hate myself more?
And contributing to my road of self-mutilation?

Suicide porn and envy of being anyone but me,
Someone beautiful, attractive and mentally stable.

I fucked up,
Again and again…

I cannot wait to die,
That is my fate.

Trying Hard

I try so hard to make you feel beautiful,
Smile and take my hand.

I thought I was in love.
What happened?
How did this feeling abruptly end?
And am I sorry?

You mean so much, obviously more to me then I to you,
Is retarded miscommunication worth this,
Giving up on what we were building?

Is it worth hurting me so badly?
So painfully bad, that I want to parish.

Nothing can change that I want to die.

No Love for G.O.D.

I sometimes wonder if loves equals pain,

Or if God is just fucking me in the ass, because I choose not to believe in him.

Does Jesus look down on me and masturbate to my sadness, my depression, my hate, my death?

Or is the Devil toying with me,
Massaging my penis through my utter discomfort of self -hate?

Or is it just I,
A suicide solider on a mission interrupted by catastrophic events designed to cause my death?

Thoughts Journal*

We walk around with our heads lost in the clouds of unrealistic

visions, a picture of life so perfect, so beautiful so right.

We fool ourselves each and everyday when the truth is

revealed and the power so strong you cannot begin to grasp it.

You fade away loosing emotion and reality on life and yourself.

Each day is a struggle. A desperate plea with yourself to stay

alive to keep yourself stable, and hold back thoughts that fuels

you for suicide.

You must get use to the idea and feeling of pain, so much pain

that death is now beautiful.

Looking in the Mirror

I look in the mirror and wonder why?
Why do I feel this way every single day?

Why do I hate myself and dream of the day I no longer exist,
And all of these feelings and problems will be taken away…

All of those people who doubt me,
I will have the last laugh,
As I slowly fade away.

Why do I inflict pain and scars on myself?
And while doing it,
Starring in the mirror?

I feel so low,
So disgusting,
In pain,
Self-hatred,
Self pity,
I have no motivation and tired all the time.
WHY?

I know I need help, I need to get through, will somebody help me?
Will anybody care, when I'm dead?

Walls are closing in

I feel that the walls are closing in around me,
Light slowly fading away,
Leaving me so I can no longer see,
There's pressure all around,
Tears, pain as I fall further down.

There's an option to this struggle,
Open wide as my lips slowly caress the muzzle.

Close my eyes and count to three,
No one can help this is my fate.
I was not strong enough to handle this.

I wasn't strong enough to beat these demons,
I think of our very first kiss,
Then I gently squeeze the trigger.

Mother son Bond

Mascara clouded front door,
This pain is getting to me,
Kill myself before it's too late,
Maybe she will see,

I'm sorry I never showed you,
My heart lets you in,
Wish it all away for you,
I'll never do it again.

Your last goodbye,
Never fading away,
And it's hard to get by,
Slowing time beginning to die.
Please mom, do not cry.

I know I screwed up,
And the reality hurts so bad,
I'm black inside,
I can no longer hide it from you.

CHAPTER 8: 2003

City Of Sadness

My life is sealed by two distinct black walls,
An interstate of racing thoughts,
Scattered throughout a city of morbid ruin.

Suicidal cells circulating,
Polluting the air of this decomposing surrounding,
Tearing holes in each brain wave.

There are many doors painting the walls,
Each an opening to a hidden reality.
On each door protrudes an industrial strength lock,
Designed to protect oneself from eternal sadness.

In a constant war with the one who holds the Key,
Whose power so strong,
Can open each and every door,
Creating a lowness of absorbing disease.

A growing desperation to be free,
To cut all power,
By destroying the one who holds the Key,
Manic Depression.

When ever presented with an unlocked door,
Shadowed memories of utter discomfort become visible.
Revealing an empty bed maintained by a broken heart.
Soon all other memories begin to surface,
Like tiny thorns imbedded into my brain.

A bottle of empty pills,
Unprotected intercourse,
An aborted fetus,
As well as many mistakes gift-wrapped in hopes of a surprise,
But instead further mental torture.

Lost in internal suffering,
And hopes to one day rebuild my city with Lexapro bricks.

MANIC DEPRESIVE LOW*

Lately I have been in one of those zones. The lows of manic depression have conquered me and I feel as that moving up is almost impossible. My veins throb and visions of slicing them open become clear. I am sad, there is no other word for it.

I feel as if in a desperate state to regain sanity and erase the images that burn so deep inside my soul. To slowly take a gun and place against my temple, pull the trigger and say goodbye to my life of mental torture, self-mutilation and inner decay. I am 19 years old and feel I am all alone. No cure and nothing works, with suicide as a soul mate. I talk to my family and a friend. The pain calms then slowly gains speed and takes me full force.

Why are relationships so hard, confusing? I miss my friends, they're in Iraq, and I hope their ok. Maybe I would feel better if Cordova was here; I miss having him around to talk to. He saved my life and though I am grateful I wish I had died. But I didn't. I just wish my medicine worked and I could live happy for a while, to just hide my feelings for a day or two. And function like a normal 19 year old man.

The Meaning Of A Word

A Shallow Heartbeat, the rhythm of a time,
Where all has phased away.

An empty slot, anticipating the return of internal energy,
Derived from true love.

Existence is pointless in the eyes of the beholder,
Strong enough to remove each feeling that allows a smile,
A handshake, even an orgasm.

I feel as if forced to contaminate myself,
In woman only interested in soiling the sheet beneath them.
To just feel whole in the moment being,
And erase the memory of enduring alone triumph.

      Pleasure induced, but mistaken for love,
      And a companion to hold in the dreadful temps
outdoors.

Must I seek a bullet- to fall in love with?
Make love and say good night to,
Or a double-edged sword to remove myself from this drama,
Of yearning to be loved,
In a world which doesn't know the meaning?

In Need Of Self Worth

Peering into a heart,
Full of emotional ruin and suicidal triumph,
Finding words to convey,
The feeling ones feels for another,
Lost in the debris,
Caused by journeys ending in broken pieces.

A black hole replacing the foundation,
Of an internal life ticker,

For how must I feel, when loosing all feeling?

One can hope to dream,
Experiencing a reality,
Non-existent to the one being lived.

Finding out what it means to love one's self,
Erase these memories,
That haunts me, forcing me to remain in this spot,
Dwelling in this self-hatred.

To slowly step into a different skin,
Intact with a soul,
Moving on to escape this sadness,
That consumes me,
        Raping my soul and changing the face I wear so
anonymously.

Kenneth J. Cody

Removing a minute of your life

I look to you when life is too hard to bear,
In my hand you are gently placed,

Lying there you decay at my fingertips,
Sizzling away at my every puff.

I enjoy inhaling you at you up most potency,
To mutilate the lungs I need all to badly.

I cannot help, but feel close to you.
Disguising yourself as a friend,
But instead Death, lingering around the corner,
As if a gun to my head, slowly squeezing the trigger.

This friendship between us is a battle I am slowly loosing,
For I depend on you,
To live,
Breath,
And even feel.

Why My Grandfather?

It's beginning to get hard to feel,
What I use to think was real,
Watching him slowly die,

Trying to release a smile,
Trying so hard to, just get by.
Why must it have to be this way?
Why can't he live another day?

I watch him try to stand up,
I watch him painfully sit down,
Watch the family all around him,
Trying not to utter a sound.

Cancer is the enemy,
An anatomy life taking tragedy,
Oh I feel I can't handle me,
When you're gone and no longer here,
Who will be there to guide thee?

DYSPHORIC MANIA*

Imagine a rabid dog, heart is beating only human. My mind was racing and it was as if all hope had been lost. I was depressed but this time was different. I didn't understand. I had racing thoughts, clammy hands, high anxiety and extreme suicidal ideation. I was screaming inside and panting on the outside, I was in hell and I wasn't dreaming. I remember wanting to sleep, hating myself and dreaming of my death.

I had pictured it many times and as I gripped my beautiful pistol I knew it was not how I had planned however if was my only option. I didn't want to die, but I didn't want to go on feeling this way. I was going insane, my depressive episodes were never this aggressive and I didn't understand. My racing thoughts were focusing on friends who no longer existed, the Army and what they had put me through.

I missed my child hood, I thought of my earlier suicide attempt and thought that had I succeeded I wouldn't be in the middle of this current nightmare. I cried out and I screamed, I smoked multiple cigarettes and ironically I did not drink. I paced around the room, the carpet shuffling beneath my feet. Why could I not sleep, if only I could to a wake to see another day?

We had just learned that my ex-sister in law was pregnant with my niece Adrianna and I thought of being an uncle, I held on to anything positive to keep myself alive and as the tear poured down my cheeks, the depression and the mania grew worse. At the time I was not aware that I was Bipolar type 1 and that I was able to have Depression and Mania together which is referred to as Dysphoric Mania. However my night grew more interesting.

I couldn't take it anymore so I slammed myself down onto the bed making a loud thud; surprisingly no one in my house awoke. Not even my little sister whose room was only ten feet away. I didn't care, maybe the added company would have supplied my mental capacity with relief, and however in this state I probably should have been hospitalized, and have since learned that this is also why the Anti-Depressant Lexapro should never be prescribed to an individual with Bipolar Disorder. While lying in my bed I decided to talk to my grandfather Michael Joseph Cody for whom we had lost recently to cancer. My grandfather was a hero of mine and to this date still is. He was a great father and grandfather and was always there for his family and this was a time where I needed him the most.

Also in light of the obvious embarrassment I had brought to my extended family with my Mental illness discharge from the United States Army, my grandfather was always my biggest supporter.

By saying I talked to my grandfather is more of an understatement; it is more like I begged to my grandfather, I begged to my grandfather to fall asleep. I lay in my bed crying profusely, with a loaded gun in my hand yearning to die. However I am here to day writing my story. I knew that if I could fall asleep I would be able to wake up and live another day.

So I begged my grandfather to help me fall asleep, my panting increased, my mania increased and this is when my first out body experience occurred and I experience Bipolar Psychosis. It started to get cold and the room grew dark and green. I felt my body begin to sink into my bed as I slowly left my room. I began to sink further down and I felt as if I was traveling to hell. It was as if the gun had discharged and I had died.

Maybe I had and god was real. Was I being repaid for the sins I had committed. Was my fate sealed and this was my entrance into hell? I didn't know but it was at this point that I began to hear a voice say, "I got to get out of this place" over and over. I cannot for the life of me tell you whose voice it was, but I can assure you there was a voice. After what felt like an eternity I felt my body begin to rise up through the green aura and back up to the bed where I was originally laying.

I then began to feel warm and as I looked to the ceiling I focused on a silhouette of a baby's face. The image was so peaceful I managed to fall asleep, which at the point was all I could have ever asked for. When I awoke the next morning the gun was lying in my crotch loaded. Had it gone off I would have instantly lost my testicles and not have been able to father my beautiful children years later. Though I woke up and surprisingly the Dysphoric mania was no longer upon me (this can last a long period of time) I however was stuck in a long depressive low.

A depressive low was the least of my worries because anyone who has ever experienced Dysphoric mania can tell you this is a very dangerous state of mind to be in. I believe that my grandfather heard me loud and clear that night and saved my life. My research has concluded that hearing voices is part of Dysphoric mania, and I have heard voices many other times in the past ten years during manic episodes, which is part of the symptoms, associated with bipolar disorder.

Symptoms such as these that coincide with other psychotic symptoms such as paranoid delusions, hallucinations, and Dysphoric mania sometimes mimic those of Schizophrenia; this is why bipolar type 1 is so similar and considered the most severe form of bipolar disorder.

Dysphoric Mania Poetic mumblings*

-I sit and feel a shadow begin to shade my face,
I glance up to see a dark cloud giving shelter to a disgraceful
human being,
Warm fluid collapses on my cheeks, but it's not rain,
It's coming from my eyes…

And though I'm sitting alone it's getting harder to breath,
In desperate need of air and nowhere to receive it,
A light gives shine and revealed is a pleasure pistol,
The temptation is there to place my hand upon its handle,
Squeeze it powerful trigger,
Close my eyes and remove myself from this scene of the
world.

-You peered into a thought,
Hoping to reveal true feelings,
Of happiness pleasure and pain but nothing exist.
A melancholy scapegoat.
A yearning, a wanting to no longer be alone.
There's a picture of you and its slowly fading away into infinite
turmoil.
Down deep underneath the casket of those like me.
Each days a determination to free, free from the grips of
bipolar.
Escape the feelings of sadness, mania, and mortal death.

Scared and uncovered,
Ashamed and derailed,
Forgive hopefully to forget,
Pain with a mental picture of it,
Deep behind my eyes of lasting suicide envy.

-A painted face,
A sour distinctive taste,

A soul not worth selling,
A fragrance not worth smelling.

A permanent depressive stain,
A mind tormented filled with pain,
Wrist needs to be slit,
Create cancer,
Keep my cigarette lit,
Suicide to touch become friends,
Erase my smile when love ends,
Slowly die,
Say goodbye,
Ashes to ashes,
Dust to dust,
Must go to hell,
If I must.

I hate you

The thought of you sends shivers down my spine,
How I can't even stand to look at you.

Trying to see into you, filtered through
Black anguish and cold heartedness.

You disgust me, making me knot up from within,
And I hope to finally throw you away.

There are no feelings worth feeling for you, to you or with you.

Nothing can be said, because of what you have accomplished.

Me wanting you to parish, eat your empty soul,
And feel the sickness you have caused.

TO BE A SOILDER*

June 2003: As I look at the photo of me in my Class A. uniform

I only feel one thing and that is pride. I only wish that my

superiors could have been more supportive of me while going

through the lows on my way out of the military. I feel guilty

knowing that my friends are overseas and here I am living up

life and playing the Rock n' Roll star.

Hidden behind tattoos that indeed reflect my personality, but

do not make me who I am. Know that you all are not forgotten.

I will always be one of you 4/1 Field Artillery. I only wish that

the circumstances could have been different. Come home

safe.

Tired of Being Tortured By You

I looked into your eyes once,
I felt tiny bumps arise once our lips met,
And now your dead to me,

Life became painless when in your presence,
 You were special and beautiful inside and out,
And now your dead to me,

You made me feel like a person,
Letting me know that I was a someone,
And now your dead to me,

I can't believe just how disturbed you are,
Even more so then I,
And now your dead to me.

When I see you, I see an empty soul,
Just a human organism taking up space,
You have become nothing to me,
You are nothing to me,

The baby doll has not shattered,
And you are now dead to me.

Falling of an Empire.

Hello.
Are you there?

Can you hear me, or am I wasting my time, talking to dead
air?

Is the anxiety taking control, creating false imaginary
conversation?
Or is this just the way of saying my voice doesn't need to be
head and you have already fallen into the hands of those who
scare me?

Do you really know what it is that you believe in, preach about
or even vote for? When taking away one right, you destroy
another and the effect is domino.

Shall I pollute myself by thinking exactly like you, keeping my
true feelings held within?
Throwing away our first amendment right and marching in a
single file line?

I can feel it, can you? I can see it, can you?

Slowly moving into a direction of red flags,
With a communist leader with a democracy front.

Would it surprise you to learn I am not alone in this
conclusion?
Arming myself, preparing to die for what I believe in?

If only more would listen, feel and see exactly what is under
the dotted line,

Unclassified to the human eye, only needing drive and
concern to find out the truth maybe you all would understand,

A young voice can hold water; don't close your eyes to 20
years old age. Or we will all wake up in a police state
surrendering our thoughts, our visions, and our history.

Another Day, Another Struggle

Why does my life have to be so tortuous?
A constant struggle to live, love and multiply…

Walking down a dark path,
Slowly strolling looking for the light.
Eagerly trying to not fall down,
And keep moving forward.

At any point you can be interrupted and your
Destination may be compromised.

For was it the gun to your head,
Or an intoxicated sheep driving to fast?

Is it written in my book of fate
To be emotionally destroyed,
Mentally sacrificed or pillaged
Taking away every last ounce of self- respect I have?

Each day is not a good day, but another day
I must force myself to bear,
In hope that the light will shine down,
And things may be a little less excruciating.

MEDICINE CLIMAX*

My mind is a pile of shit. Thousands of little maggots feeding off the memories I try to hard to forget. I take my medicine, not the cure. Only to dope my senses into loosing grasp on reality and myself. 100 mg, 200 mg now 300 mg and soon 450 mg. What is wrong with me?

How can someone be so fucked up? Or am I just reading more into it then I really should? There's a bullet out there maybe it has my name on it. I try all so hard to find it with no luck. However one day I fear I will find it and my misery will climax and end and so will these damn mixed episodes.

There's people out there I love so much, I only wish I could love myself a quarter of what I put out to others. Anyways enough feeling sorry for myself, this depression shall pass, looking for to the up swing.

Anatomy of a Life taking Tragedy

Collapsing in sight of what looks to be you,
Deranged, mentally destroyed and loosing your grip,
Feeling your hand knowing not what to do,
Saying goodbye, with a kiss to your lip.

My eyes were blinded by tears of sorrow,
Hands trembling, a mind that didn't understand,
Asking the cancer why I can't see you tomorrow,
Clouded images, revealing suicide contraband.

I know you want me to be young and live on,
Take care of your wife and future generation,
But it's so hard now that you're gone,
You were the backbone of our family, leader of our nation,

Now its today and I can't help but miss you,
The fact you're now gone, has not yet sunk through

Various mumbles during cigarette smoking*

- There I am, sitting by myself and I can't remember what I was doing there. Time passes by, and I'm sickened by the thought of what's been done before.

- Taking my time thinking of life. How close I had come to entering a world unlike the one we live in today playing with fire, dancing with my aborted fetus, me.

- Vision has ceased as you travel down a cold dark road or mortal pain and vile Armageddon. It grows hard to move, desperate to think and impossible to feel.

- Finding comfort in an imaginary silhouette what could be your one true love. There's no way of knowing if your life has meaning or is it disappearing without warning? To destructive to go on, to alone to be alone. And for once have a soul, which has already been sold.

- If we could predict the future, life would be much simpler, pain would be limited, and emptiness would soon be rewarded. There would be no question of what path to travel, what would be ok to feel, and who truly loves you.

Mans best family member

I close my eyes entering a different world,
A world that only dreams are made of.
As the hours tick pass my life travels many different
paths,
I am suddenly awaken,

back to a mortal reality of decomposition.

His eyes so innocent,
His size so small.

I am fascinated at the fact that this little defenseless
creature
Could be full of so much love as well as devotion for
me.

When opening the door to my bedroom,
He quickly runs to his water dish.
I release a smile hearing his little dog tags rattling
together,
And the sound of his little paws tapping the kitchen
floor.

His anticipation grows as I make it closer to the back
door.
To us using the bathroom is no big deal,
but to a 12 lb. Bichon you are truly a god.
And opening that door is worth a thousand licks.

He feeds off affection, and licks our tears away.

When accompanied by this creature,
We are indeed reminded that true he is mans best
friend, But a family member he has become.

Suicidal Ideation

It's cold and my skin is bare,
Tempt me not if you dare,
There's a bottle of pills it looks so good,
All my actions have been misunderstood.

I've got a gun and maybe I'll use it,
That's just one more option,
Should I abuse it?

How about that sharp knife,
For the fatal final slice,
Do it right the first time,
Was always helpful advice.
In a time like this is so hard to go on.
Will anyone miss me when I'm gone?

Will anyone care when my face is destroyed,
Wrist slit head clipped,
Body deployed over a bridge face down in the water,

Body drained of all life so happy to die,
Never say goodbye,
My outside actions were all a lie.

Don't ask me why,
It's too late I'm done I'm finished, through the end of story,
So when you feel I was lying,
Wallowing in self-pity,
Just remember you should have believed me.

Beginning to Fall

My hand is trembling,
My eyes slowly try to focus,
My heartbeat cannot be controlled.

And I'm being torn,
My outer shell that once was exposed,
Has disappeared revealing a more me.

Trying so hard to keep the rain from projecting from my eyes.

Your soul untouched and unsaved 1998

I try,
Sometimes I feel I try a little too hard,
Like when the music stops and I have become a gleaming star,

I listen,
I see,
I hear the things you preach to me.

I beg,
I cry,
When all has been left and its time to say goodbye.
Come here,
If I go then stay,
I sit all calm depression clouds me,
Trying to get inside of me.

I kiss your lips for the last time,
Never did anything,
Loving you was my only crime.

Hey it's now over,
Hey it's now over and gone.

Low

The pressure begins to grow,
As I feel my lungs begin to tighten,
Breathing becomes limited and I'm slowly
fading into sadness unlike no other,
I no longer look to a gun,
But a teddy bear,
Reminding myself of the comfort of not being alone,

An emptiness,
Not a suffering,
A want to live,
Not a yearning to die and leave the world.
How can I express to you how I feel when you do not exist?

CHAPTER 9: Melissa 2004

MEETING MELISSA

The day I met Melissa the timing could not have been better. I had sworn off relationships and decided that in order to be in a successful relationship and be able to truly give myself to someone; I needed to be able to fix myself first. I was going down a really bad path. I was hanging out with individuals who enjoyed the same things in life I currently enjoyed.

I stayed out late getting drunk and high went to school during the day and didn't have a care in the world. Relationships were the last thing on my mind due to the pain that I had suffered, and substance abuse seemed like a better alternative at the time.

However, the day I met Melissa all of that had changed. It was the first day of school of the school year and I had gone to school to switch a class that year. I walked in the back entrance of the school and as I walked in I saw Melissa sitting on the sofa over by the soda machines. I thought she was beautiful. As I looked over at her I knew instantly she was going to be my wife, I cannot explain how I knew but I knew instantly.

I thought of an excuse to go over there and noticed that sitting near her was a guy who was tattooed and pierced as I was and figured they were friends. By going over there to purchase as soda I figured that the guy would see me and initiate a conversation, which would then lead to a way for me to be introduced to Melissa. As I walked over to the soda machines I was completely nervous and I could feel their eyes watching me walk towards them and I remember think to myself "I better not trip".

Upon getting over to the soda machine the guy with the tattoos and the piercings initiated a conversation as predicted and his name turned out to be Jesse. Jesse and I hit off immediately and fortunately he in fact was acquaintance with Melissa and he introduced me to her. I grabbed a soda and suggested having a cigarette knowing that smoking was my vice and a way for me to relax while creating a discussion. My plan worked and before I knew it Melissa and I were heavy in discussion, neglecting Jesse and his other friend that tagged along.

That day Melissa and I exchanged phone numbers and before I arrived home Melissa had already called me. I took this as a good sign and knew that fate had shown it hailing light upon me and I better not screw this up. That night I called Melissa and we spoke on the phone for hours on end about poetry and past relationships and family. We instantly connected and I knew then that the initial feeling I had when I first saw her was true and real and that she in fact would eventually be my wife, I only knew her for two days by this point but I knew we were to be.

I loved the fact that she was a mother to Courtney then 5 months old and Courtney was her whole world. Melissa had her head on straight and was a nursing student. I was a washed out soldier recovering for a torn heart and mental breakdown, suffering with a new diagnose of bipolar disorder (a year old) at this point. I was parting and skipping class and she was squared away. I knew to be with her I needed to get my shit together. I remember Melissa telling me that I was a cool kid and she really liked me, but she had left one drunk already and wanted a good environment for her daughter. She saw the potential in me. When she told me that I curbed my ways and straightened up.

The feelings I had for Melissa at that point were so strong that I was willing to change and change is what I did, and the rest is history. Two months later on November 12, 2005 I took Melissa out to dinner and asked her to marry me. We had only been dating for a little over two months. Melissa said yes and I explained to her that I would be the father to Courtney that Courtney needed.

May 22, 2005 on my Grandmother's birthday Melissa and I were married, I had our wedding vowels altered in order to incorporate Courtney into the ceremony in order to honor her and pledge my devotion to being her daddy for the rest of my life; Melissa and I had only been dating a little over 7 months. As I sit here and write this book Suffering in Silence, Melissa and I have been together eight years and married seven of them. We share a home and four beautiful children together.

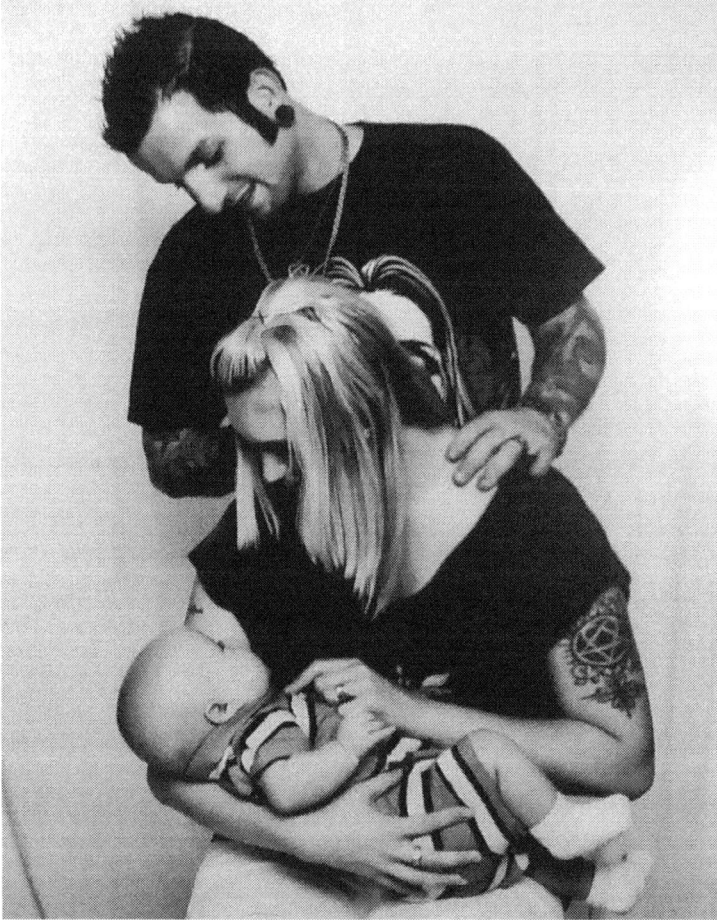

(Me with Melissa and Kenny 2012).

Feeling Real...

When I kiss, I begin to feel,
The effects of her, I begin to heal,
A suicidal climax, you cannot steal,
Not an 8 inch solider, needed to seal,

The commitment of what looks to be love,

A smile, a whisper,
A sweet spot between her thighs,
An unconditional conversation,
Before we realize, the time flies by,

You make me feel so unashamed,
I make love to you,

And realize I am human,
a tiger slowly being tamed, and

Falling in love and saying hello,
for we will never depart,

For I will never let you go.

New Smile

Looking in the mirror,
Reflecting on what looks to be real,
Though you don't feel sad,
Your wombs have begun to heal,

Your crippled hand,
The revolver it once caressed,
Has found it place under the stand,

These tears that fall,
They are falling from my love,
My love that once was empty,
And I am now at piece.

I love you.

A touch of dialogue

I entered a house,
A house that was empty,
My life stood still,
As the stars began to brighten,

The world had become ours.

When I peered into your eyes,
For the first time,
A connection was born,
I was unaware I was falling in love.

You looked past my painted canvas,
Through this distorted me,
And into my soul;
We had then become whole.

I knew just then you were the one,
The one you see in fiction cardboard cut outs,
Torn pages with a touch of scarlet,
Flower petals and then a smile.

This time I was alive.

One Month

Your tenderness is what attracts my heart to your flower,
How I only wish to explore your insides,
Ponder through each and every one of your body parts,
Explore each of your taste,
And pleasure you wet.

My heart is opened for you,
How I must reveal myself,
And totally quiver in your presence.

Love with you needs no word such as fuck,
For this will be an adventure of pure pleasure,
And safety for your token you choose to give to me.

How I bleed needing it all to badly…

   One month from now may change both our lives.

Two Stars, Two Companions

A star shining so bright,
Its radiant tranquility absorbing into your essence,
Emotionally gripping the inside of your person.

When all is alone,
This star sits all alone,
Except a little star right beside it,
A lot smaller in size but just as beautiful.

These stars mesmerize me,
Constantly encompassing my mind,
Swallowing my thoughts,
Creating internal bliss and a warmth unlike no other.

I find myself wanting to move closer to these stars,
A journey sought out but not planned,
My heart pumps so hard when looking into the sky.

Seeing this star, her sidekick and kissing her sweet lips.

I only wish and imagine my place in the sky beside them,
Her, and you…

Life is becoming bliss,
And I am becoming real.

Bipolar Aura of Marriage

The sky was dark swallowing the shadow of death,
Mimicked by the impression of your being,

Collapsing itself in your green aura,
Hibernating inside your shell.

Looking through a distorted vase seeing the beauty
within its essence,
Truly loving,
Though the flower has passed away.

Hitching your heart to mine...

The love highway has been empty from time to time,
An emptiness that was there before you.

Our missions the same,
You by my side,
Embracing your true beauty,
As you had do for me.

I love you Melissa until the end,
Forever we are one.

You Saved Me

I once lay in my bed,
Contemplating the life I use to live,
I had grown hollow.

A cold resemblance of what I once was,
Had plagued the shell of a mind that yearned to be destroyed.

My eyes had now dried,
After releasing an overwhelming waterfall of painful memories.

I wished for her,
A person to complete the heart I wore so disgracefully upon
my shoulder.

At a point where nothing could be felt,
Numb,
Decaying from the pain I had felt for so long.

You intrigue me,
And give everything I always wanted to feel.

I can't resist a smile when in your presence,
I can no longer feel the sensation of self-mutilation,
There are no words that can describe you.

My six-foot hole is slowly being filled,
Maybe its time to feel again,
To love,
And be happy.

Your Eyes

When looking into your eyes a warmth consumes me,
Shading my face, and penetrating my soul.

How can feelings other then love and devotion be shared with
her,
The one with those eyes.

Although I wish you felt no pain in your short years,
I am grateful for bad memories brought us together.

And a feeling within my insides is being felt,
For you have opened a door which once was locked.

And created a spot for my broken heart,
As you slowly nurse it back to original form.

Only this time its stronger and more sincere,
       You are my every thing.

CHAPTER 10: 2004

Your Skin has feeling

His canvas is pasty,
Cold and unforgiving.

Vomiting due to its existence,
Covering his blood like an icy blanket.

His canvas is weeping,
Begging to be left alone.

Leave me be,
For I am not your enemy.

With waves breaking without warning,
His eyes are saturated in the ocean..

Created subconsciously from the craters,
Burnt into his canvas randomly,

He knows not what he does,
Only that the pain disappears each moment.

Self-infliction.

Determined to destroy his inner self,
Only to torture his canvas, which is innocent.

Pick me up, beginning to fall

I feel the walls closing in,
The light flickers then disappears,
Silence is present and I'm fading away.

Nothing is right it is always so wrong,
My insides are hollow and my stability is affected.

I am running out of gas on a deserted highway,
There's thunder and lightning but it will not rain,
My tears make up for the lack of moisture.

I am sinking, please help for I cannot bear to fall further down.

Looking for Wisdom

When reflecting on oneself, one can imagine until their hearts
content,
A world such as the one in which they live,
Or another creating a picture perfect reality,
Where they no longer feel the burden of pain,
Living with constant racing thoughts,
Emotions changing the effects of one's life,
In hopes to close your eyes and see the stars.

Nothing feels right with everything always hurting,
Except looking into the sky.

Untitled

Sitting in the shadow facing a locked door,
The display of self-mutilation flashing before my eyes,
A shallow gasp.

Ventilation is being prevented,
And a mysterious light peers through a crack in the ceiling,
Mystery echoes,
Decisions masturbate my mind,
Climaxing is impossible,
Suicide is no longer an option,
Faced with a conflict I cannot run nor hide,
To make a decision I am separated from reality,
An out of body experience.

And the pain eases away.

Random*

Our minds reflecting our essence we choose to reveal to the
ones who are interested,

Sculpting an imaginary garden,
Making love to a bright blue sky,
Surrounded by hypocrites pretending to be humans,

Painting false smiles,
Glowing in the howling wind.

Slathered words arranged purposely to unscrew the working
minds,
Falsifying hidden details in which are too important to deny,
But blind to the naked eye,
And we all awake in a burning bed,
Cake in feces of burning propaganda.

Eat me away

I cannot begin to relate to a time when I was free,
From you, me as well as everybody,
A constant struggle to maintain breathing,
An everlasting cycle through a personal hell.

Been told thing so true,
So real and so pure,
I'm so eager to relax and remove this substance,
Swooshing around bleeding my eyes destroying my heart.

Why do I constantly beg to die,
Wanting nothing more but to rot,
Allowing the maggots to eat away my mortality,
In hopes of being reborn into a world that understands me.

Going down far

Contemplating my fate,
Sweat anxiety ridden solider,
On his way to more mental self-inflicted torture.

A final decision so strong and painful.

Only asking for love,
Show me love,
Express it,
Let it evolve and I will embrace it.

It's so late in the game,
To screwed up with no controlled substance and alone.

Why the picture can't be revealed,
An image blurred distorted by curiosity and anger,
Sadness,
What caused the past and created the future.

On the verge of another breakdown.

To balance I make love to a lit object,
A cancer stick so addicting, so tasteful and pleasurable.

I wear my permanent wounds, self-inflicted, tear infested
suicide symbolic statement.

I sometimes wish my overdose ended in death why did I have
to wake up to live another day.

CHAPTER 11: 2005

I Will Watch You Grow

Why am I in the position?
A constant fear of saying goodbye?
Letting go of your smile,
Forever deteriating from your "Da, Da…"

Seeing you awaken from your nap,
A tinkle in your eyes;

And then a kiss…
Baby's breath, with a touch of your voice.

I take you as my own,
Watching you grow;
Learning something new each and everyday.
Only to hear that the other part of you now cares.

I tell myself he's to late,
You call me daddy though,
My love for you sweet princess;
Is more then I could ever explain.

I am your dad,
 Your other half wasn't there.

I have raised you as my own,
So where was he?

Its not you fault I feel so sad,
How could I ever explain to you?
Money was the match that lit his fire,
And I am burning right now.

My little angel I tell you,

I will watch you grow.
Although I am scared of loosing you,
You will always be my daughter, I your dad.

My Beretta

I look at you,
I see black,

Small and slender,
Possessing a grip like no other.

Your texture so smooth,
A smell so refreshing;
Gunpowder caressing my nostrils.

A .40 caliber pistol,
Initiating a kick with each trigger pull,
Though easy to handle.

I dreamed of you,
Since I was a little boy,
Having you as my Lethal Weapon.

Squeezing you,
Controlling you.

Holding you in my hands.

Just a Tattoo

The imagery is immaculate,
A radiance of red,
Black never looked so peaceful,
As the needle plunges our casing.

A mark of the beast,
Tampering our skin,
Slowly releasing an exhale,
As an outline appears.

A blob of ink,
Trash to the naked eyes,
When wiped away a story is told.
A feel of relief,
And eager for just one more.

Expressing what you feel,
Bleeding to cater our flesh,
Taken back to ones youth,
Coloring in a coloring book.

And image is relevant.

In the Morning

Lying there,
Tossing and turning,
Engulfed in racing thoughts.

Wishing the clock was wrong.

Having to awake,
From a sleep never slept,
Feeling as though I am gone.

Locked away,
From what is real,
Only to walk along in my broken shoes.

When walking,
It's not a walk,
Nearly a shuffle towards the sink.

Past the loaded gun
　　　That's only feet away…

A mission of water,
Grasping the counter turning the knob.
A cool liquid to cleanse these bleeding eyes.

　　　Pain,
　　　So much pain,
　　　Up and down my spine,
　　　It begins to befriend my tear ducts.

Reaching for my lighter,
Inhibiting the air around me,
Griping my Marb. With anticipation.

Spark a Spark and inhale,
   Now this is life…

Far From Heaven

The room is murky,
Although flames burn.

No light is uncovered.
Sinister.

A feeling of panic,
Emerges unwillingly.

The sounds of chains
rattle the door.

As if someone were near.

Moans,
So many moans.
Hundreds of whips snaps,
With each snap; another moan.

A disgusting example of true brutality.

Begging for freedom,
Yearning to be free.

Among the flames,
A chair arises.
Releasing a metal claw gripping into your side,
Like a magnet to metal.

Your energy quickly drains,
As your trying to escape this force.
Gripping the claw,
Only to remove corroded blood.

Escape is impossible,
Moving towards the flames.
Finding yourself being strapped to this chair,
Burning for eternity.

Engulfed in Mania

I am reaching the end,
Of the grasp you hold.

Struggling, weeping;
Begging to go on.

So much anger,
Oozing through bleeding fingernails.

This rage comes,
Then slowly retreats.

Always wondering
Why can I not smell the flowers?

Flowing…

Dripping…

Further down the spiral,
Eating away at my insides.

Erasing my memory,
Of being happy.

Continuing to fall;
Down,

Down.

Internal Falling

I was moving up, then falling down.
A constant fight to stay constant.

Why can't it be set in stone,
An agenda, a schedule; a feeling.

Hurting those I love.
Especially you,
Placing my emotional baggage on your shoulders.

I still smile; I just wish I no longer felt,
I am going nowhere.

Awaken from being awake,
Sick from being sick.

I close my eyes, feeling for the remote.
Changing a channel,
Only to realize this channel cannot be changed.

Releasing a tear;
And kissing your lips.

Comfort me.

Manic

The eyes so dark,
A face so broken.
Bounded by course pasty skin,
Darkened by a dismal mist.

Walking with two legs,
An animal forgotten to most;
But not this day.

Twitching.

Begging for life to loosen its grip,
For its mind to relax.
Falling asleep, only to awake.

Stalking another day.

I know you're out there pt. 1

Was it you who saved me that night?
The light in the sky,
When the sky was painted black?

The below freezing temperature,
A blanket of snow;
Distorting the road.

I knew it was you as I lit my cigarette,
Placed my foot on the gas;
In a vehicle with no brakes.

You knew I was naïve to what winter was like here,
A constant blur to a young runner,
In a new climate.

You saved my life.

Didn't you? Pt. 2

I knew it was you,
Who made me warm?

When I cursed the sky,
Gripping my heart, shedding those tears.

How I begged for you,
To help me fall asleep.

You saw didn't you?
The gun placed to my head?

You felt the pain the I was enduring,
And you knew I really wanted to live?

I fell asleep that night.

A life taker lying beside me.

I had changed thanks to you.
You had again saved my life.

And I am grateful.

Chapter 12: 2006

I forgave my brother

Alone in the corner of a well lit room,
Squeezing my fist tightly together.
Tears releasing themselves,
As I pray for a shadow to shade my being;

Allowing me to go unseen.

The torment given by an older sibling,
Whose purpose is not to play;
But to abuse you until no end.
Realizing you're not a brother,
But a permanent fixture to pounce on.

To go outside, your tongue must lick his shoe,
Kiss his ass, just before licking the urine stained toilet seat.
Sore to the touch from the punishment he's given you,
And the teachers were always asking questions.

Especially the time the gold chain lay next to the heater,
Amusing himself, he placed it around my neck.
The melted scar created a circumference around my throat.

For years I was his mule,
His lab rat of experiments.

Blisstex up my nose,
Choking on toilet paper.

Binacca breath spray
Burning my rectum.

And a gang beating by all of his friends
Enforcing an initiation for a grade I was not in.

Growing up to be a loaded weapon,
Hot headed and fueled to fight.
I finally forgave him when our grandfather died.

To: little M.

I must say,
It's nice to say hello to you.
I must say that though I cannot see you,
I know you are there.

You know I am not so naïve anymore.
Raising your sister and ready to raise you,
True bliss.

I know now I lived because of you.
I was a lonely soul,
In a world which had not yet been created for you.
I now know I was wrong to try and kill myself,
For that would have deleted you.

I hope those intestinal drug induced spasm pills I swallowed
haven't affected you the way they affected me,

It amazes me that I could love you so much; knowing we have
not yet met,

See I am your daddy, and I am happy you didn't see me wish
to end my existence.

Destroying the world you hadn't seen yet, there I go again
repeating myself, just ask your sister about how daddy repeats
himself.

I use to fall asleep those days with no reason, no reason at all.
I now realize the reason was you. As your co- creator I needed
to survive in order for you to live. I cannot wait until your
birthday,

I will be there crying.

A King, but not today

A breeze blowing through his mane,
The lion is roaming about.

He is looking for his cub,
Checking far and wide.

No stone is left unturned.

He's a king that has no rules,
Sneaking from here to there,
Is all too strange.

A game to be played with his daughter,
His title is not king, but daddy.

Reaching a horizon,
A shadowed figure of her,
Appears in front of him.

He's got her!

Licking a kiss, on her cheek.
A father and a teacher too.

Smiling as he lets out a loud roar!
"I love you daddy, you a lion", she replies.

"I love you too", I say looking down at her, from all fours.

The Road to fate

The night is silent, not a whistle nor a branch,
Can be heard… even in the distance.

The moons casting a crimson glow reflection,
Filter less from the macabre,
The day's activities have created.

A road usually so black,
Except for the reddish tar liquid,
Splattered throughout.

Tonight.

Revealing through the saturated pavement,
Mirroring the dark sky above,
Tiny particles of glass,
Parallel the millions of stars from beyond.

The fire of hell erupts from the vehicle,
Heating the liquid,
Slowly bringing it to a boil,
As if it's running through the veins,
 It once swam within.

There's no life,
Only the remains of two,
The driver stuck in the seat belt,
Whose mouth is still open,

A perfect portrait of burning death.

And the passenger tattooed by stars,
The windshield was nice enough to pay for,
Faced down on the pavement,

Calling home to say goodbye, Only to find there's no answer.

And they rolled on

A confused disease ridden clunk,
Swallowing his holy majesty to stay alive,
Confining their ignorance, in a crucifix trunk.

Ripping away at society each and every chunk,
Swarming all over like a gigantic beehive,
A confused disease ridden clunk,

Moving about, intoxicating the air like a rabid skunk,
On television, soaps and porn they teeter and dive,
Confining their ignorance in a crucifix trunk.

Yearning for control of the sick and the drunk,
A mission for heaven they continue to strive,
A confused disease ridden clunk.

Creeping and crawling out a hole or from a tree trunk,
Polluting the minds of those who survive,
Confining their ignorance in a crucifix trunk.

Collecting souvenirs, made from our petty junk,
However powerful they have become they only slowly thrive,
A confused diseased ridden clunk,
Confining their ignorance in a crucifix trunk.

Having an average wallet

What am I?
A man?
A sinner?
No, just an average trying to hold on.

Trying all so hard to escape the tyranny of you.
A piece of paper,
Distorted green stamped with a happy face.

A diabolical tool, forcing humans over the edge.
Druggies standing in line to buy a gun,
Only to hinder ones life to capture the dead presidents.

Or just an average at a loss for words,
Preparing to leap off a bridge to erase their burden.

Transpire from your castle,
A bank with so much power,
Fueled by those with skinny smiles,
Perfect credit and a six-figure income.

Leaping over those in need to feed their starvation,
For high class automobiles,
Million dollar homes with pleasant dreams,
Falsified as our hero's.

This adversary of human kind,
Stealing our souls,
Masturbating to our design,
With no climax in sight,
I burn you and curse your core.

Chapter 13: Recent Times

Bipolar Awareness Entry 8/22/12

So Topamax finally cut through the severe mania I had for over a month plus with irritability, then I went into a three-week depressive spell, then 4 plus weeks of mixed episodes equals scary (I now understand why hospitalization was recommended). Then a few days of normal mood and I could not believe how wonderful it felt to have my mind back. Day four of hypomania (feels wonderful) I'm addicted and the reason I got off meds again to begin with. However I have learned my lesson.

Looking forward to adding Abilify to my cocktail. I'm bipolar type 1, and this site has helped me begin to open up. I enjoy having a place to come when I cannot sleep and no one to call, and the wife's asleep and I cannot sleep, lol.

I love being able to not feel alone, and know there are others out there. At work it gets embarrassing, I work in customer service and today I was talking so fast I had to repeat myself a thousand times. I want so badly to explain why, but I can't. I have to hold it all in. Drives me nuts you know. Oh yeah has anyone had the peripheral shadows of Death, that's what I call them. They come at you from the left and the right?

The Monster Sleeps Inside

Wallowing through the darkness,
Muttering words of forgives,

The pain I've caused,
The tears I've cried,

The monster sleeps inside.

I cannot help but feel,
The fear of what might happen tomorrow,
Please believe me when I say I'm sorry in advance,

I love you until the end.

Goodnight…

Med Adjustment

Shuffling through the day,
Existing in the sun,
A cloud upon your shoulders,
Wondering when the time will come.

For the burden to ease,
Your mind to settle,
And the tension to fade.

A capsule to make you tall,
one to make you small.

Living an existence such as this,
Breathing a day such as this,
Living a moment such as this,
When will the feeling change?

The monster hides for the time being,
Leaving behind a layer of uncontrollable sigh,
Hyper tension depressive convulsion explosion;
Adjusting the end of time.

Just Mommies Web Post By Melissa M. Cody*

Another OT but kind of of related - I had posted a bit ago, that I was preoccupied with DH and trying to get him on track with his Bipolar disorder. I am pleased to say that he is much more stable, and his meds have finally started to become therapeutic. While I was on bed rest with Kenny, he worked so hard at running the household and keeping the girls on schedule and making sure they could see me daily. Trying to maintain as much normalcy while life wasn't normal, that he had neglected himself :(

The day I called him to let him know he needed to get

to the hospital because I was hemorrhaging he was faced with

his worst fears, potentially losing me and Kenny. At 1 minute,

Kenny's Apgar's were 1. And I had lost 2 liter's of blood. When

we were both okay, DH suffered a break. He struggled silently

with it until he couldn't anymore :(Thank you again ladies for

being here to listen, to read and post and txt when I needed it.

You all were extremely helpful to me getting through that

rough time ♥ -Melissa

New Doctor, a new start* 9/21/12

So today I met with my new doctor. What's cool about this is I have only ever gone to the walk in clinic because ever since my very first bipolar diagnoses I have never really trusted a doctor. In the military my first doctor diagnosed me and then betrayed my confidence. When I was discharged my original psych. Evaluation and diagnoses had disappeared and I was discharged with Borderline Personality Disorder. What a stigma that diagnoses brings.

All in all the appointment went well and I really like the doctor I met today. He let me talk and let out a good portion of my story. Due to time constraints and the fact that we will be meeting on a regular basis, I was not able to tell him my life story. I left with an addition to my Bipolar type 1/ mixed diagnose.

The addition that was added is rapid cycling, which completely explains a lot. I am even happier to have a doctor who is not afraid to use the diagnoses rapid cycler because those in the Psychiatric field will tell you that is a very controversial diagnosis. So the verdict with me official is Bipolar Type 1 with severe mixed episodes and rapid Cycling.

I look forward to telling my doctor my story and opening up. I opened up about my hallucinations, paranoia, and manic episodes. It felt refreshing considering this is his job you know. I'm sure with the exception of Melissa; the people around me can only handle so much of this topic and frankly are probably sick of it.

This man gets paid to talk about it and it feels good to get it out. Until next time,

Ken.

Bipolar Awareness Post:

So yesterday I went and met with my new doctor. It was confirmed what I had already expected. Having bipolar type 1 with psychotic episodes/ severe mixed episodes and being off meds for the past two years I have now developed rapid cycling. Needless to say I have a pretty severe diagnoses. This has been the ultimate wake up call. Where we go from here it upping my anti-psychotic, then we will up my mood stabilizer, and then possibly add a second mood stabilizer. I feel positive, after waking up.

However yesterday I was in a funk feeling low about letting myself get this way. I can no longer live in the past thinking about what I should have done differently. However the rapid cycling explains why normal mood seems to no longer exist, or at least no exist but for short periods of time. I just want my normal self- back.

FEARS*

As a man suffering from bipolar type 1, my biggest fear is getting old. I wonder what kind of man I will become as I age. Will I become mean and how bad will my episodes get as the symptoms worsen. I am already a rapid cycler and I am scared. I have read that I am facing early onset dementia and I am fearful for what my wife Melissa will be facing as far as when it pertains to taking care of me.

I made a promise to Melissa that I will continue to manage my disorder through medications, and therapy in order to stay on track and hopefully prevent or prolong the potential risk factors that go with the aging process and bipolar disorder. I am also fearful of the statistic that is one in four people with bipolar commit suicide. Will I be one of the four?

It's easy to say no, but when the disorder takes over and you want to die, it so hard to regain control. I have been there twice and attempted it. What if this disorder wins next time if there is a next time? I am scared and this is why I will never be off my meds again. I have a wife I want to grow old with and four beautiful children I want to watch grow, I have to be strong for them and survive. I also need to be there for them god forbid one genetically gets my disorder.

(Me and Kenny 2012).

THOUGHTS 10/12/12*

For the past 3 weeks I was in a depressive low. My prescribing doctor had increased my Abilify to 10 mg, and I felt things slowly starting to sink. My schoolwork started to suffer, my work started to suffer, fortunately my wife understood. It was days like this I wished for manic episode. However I was happy that things have slowed down and I was able to get some sleep. Also I was happy that there were no negative thoughts as far as suicide was concerned.

During that time period I was sitting in the mall in Concord NH and was on the brink of an anxiety attack and my daughter Courtney tells me to remember the mental health bracelet on my wrist. And to remember what it stands for daddy, she sees that I'm hurting, she sees that I'm in pain but in her 8-year-old mind its her way of telling me she understands and I love her for that.

ABOUT THE AUTHOR

I was born in Virginia and currently reside in New Hampshire with my wife Melissa and our four beautiful children. I hold a BA in Psychology and am pursuing a MBA in Human Resource Management from Southern NH University.

I was diagnosed with Bipolar Disorder Type 1 with mixed episodes and rapid cycling. Suffering in Silence documents, through 16 years of poetry, journal entries and autobiographical short stories, the trials and tribulations of bipolar disorder and how its power once dominated my life and almost destroyed my existence.

Through medication, psychotherapy, and the writing of this book, I have begun to reestablish my own place in the world and beat this disease. I will no longer stay quiet and hold it all in, and I will no longer suffer in silence.

Left to right: (Mikayla, Courtney, Kenny and Caelyn 2012).